¡Bienvenidos!
¡Welcome!

A Handy Resource Guide
for Marketing Your Library to Latinos

Susannah Mississippi Byrd

FOREWORD BY

Carol Brey-Casiano

AMERICAN LIBRARY ASSOCIATION • CHICAGO, ILLINOIS
IN COLLABORATION WITH CINCO PUNTOS PRESS • EL PASO, TEXAS

COPYRIGHT ACKNOWLEDGMENTS
Elturk, Ghada Kanafani. "Public Libraries and Improved Service to Diverse Communities,"
from *Library Services to Latinos: An Anthology*, ed. Salvador Güereña
(Jefferson, North Carolina and London: McFarland & Company, Inc., 2000).
Copyright © 2000 by Ghada Kanafani Elturk.
Sections of this work used by permission of the author.

Elturk, Ghada. "Diversity and Cultural Competency," from *Colorado Libraries* (Winter 2003): 5-7.
Copyright © 2000 by Ghada Elturk. Sections of this work used by permission of the author.

"Spanish-Language Publishing Marketplace Directory," from *Críticas, An English Speaker's Guide
to the Latest Spanish Language Titles*, online at www.criticasmagazine.com.
Copyright © 2005 by Reed Business Information. Sections of this work used by permission of the editor.

The paper used in this publication meets the minimum requirements of American National Standard
for Information Sciences—Permanence of Paper for Printed Library Materials, ANSI Z39.48-1992. ∞

Book design— JB Bryan / La Alameda Press.

Library of Congress Cataloging-in-Publication Data

Byrd, Susannah Mississippi, 1971-
Bienvenidos! = Welcome! : a handy resource guide for marketing your
library to Latinos / Susannah Mississippi Byrd ; foreword by Carol
Brey-Casiano.
p. cm.
Includes bibliographical references.
ISBN 0-8389-0902-7
1. Hispanic Americans and libraries. 2. Libraries—Special
collections—Hispanic Americans. 3. Children's libraries—Services to
Hispanic Americans. I. Title: Welcome!. II. Title.

Z711.92.H56B97 2005
027.6'3--dc22
2005006315

Printed in the United States of America

09 08 07 06 05   5 4 3 2 1

Published by the American Library Association, Chicago, Illinois
ALA Editions, 50 East Huron Street, Chicago, Illinois 60611-2795
1-866-746-7252   www.alastore.ala.org
In collaboration with
Cinco Puntos Press, 701 Texas, El Paso, Texas 79901
1-800-566-9072   www.cincopuntos.com

¡Bienvenidos!
¡Welcome!

Acknowledgments

I want to thank the following people for their time, their ideas and for their work in making libraries belong to everyone.

Martha Andrade, El Paso REFORMA Chapter

Ligia A. Arguilez, Assistance to ALA President, Carol Brey-Casiano

Yolanda Cardenas-Parra, Library Circulation Section Supervisor at the City of Commerce Public Library in Commerce, California

Lynn Coyle, Attorney, El Paso, Texas

Cathy DuPre, Media Specialist at the Collinswood Language Academy in Charlotte, North Carolina

Ghada Kanafani Elturk, Outreach Librarian at the Boulder Public Library in Boulder, Colorado

Dana Eness, Associate Director of Prime Time Family Reading Time™ at the Louisiana Endowment for the Humanities in New Orleans, Louisiana

Desiree Fairooz, Youth Librarian at the East Berry Branch Library in Fort Worth, Texas

Jack Galindo, Public Relations Coordinator at the El Paso Public Library in El Paso, Texas

Linda Garcia, Children's & Outreach Librarian for the Omaha Public Library System, South Branch in Omaha, Nebraska

Loida Garcia-Febo, Spanish Language Collections/Cultural Arts Manager for the New Americans Program at Queens Library in Jamaica, New York

Jeanette Larson, Youth Services Manager at the Austin Public Library in Austin, Texas

Larry D. Maynard, Spanish Outreach Coordinator at the Glendale Public Library in Glendale, Colorado

Maria Mena, Youth Services Coordinator at the LeRoy Collins Leon County Public Library in Tallahassee, Florida

Cathay Reta, Literacy Consultant and Statewide Project Director for Prime Time in California

José Ruiz-Álvarez, President of REFORMA National 2004-2005

Martha Toscano, Literacy Coordinator for El Paso Public Library

Rose Treviño, Youth Services Coordinator of Houston Public Library in Houston, Texas

Norma Pountney, Manager for the Omaha Public Library System, South Branch in Omaha, Nebraska

Contents

Foreword

"The library I grew up in was my only link to the outside world."
—*Playwright and filmmaker Luis Valdez*

THIS book grew out of the mutual passion that author Susannah Byrd and I share for providing Latino populations with full access to the wonderful world of libraries, information and knowledge. We live in El Paso, Texas, a unique community of approximately 750,000 people living on the U.S.-México border, where I currently serve as the Director of the El Paso Public Library.

El Paso represents everything that I celebrate as a person, and as a librarian. I love our diverse, multicultural, multilingual, binational community, and believe it is a microcosm of what our nation will someday (soon) become. Diversity is at the heart of our nation today, and for that reason must be at the heart of the library profession as well. I believe that our library personnel, collections, programs and services must reflect the diversity of our communities.

My interest in working with Latino populations goes all the way back to my high school years, when I made my first trip to México at the age of 14. After three years of Spanish class with *mi maestra* Carol Spencer, I felt ready to converse with anyone in San Miguel de Allende and México City, the two locations we visited during that two-week class trip. I had fallen in love with México and its language, and already knew that someday, I would be back. I never dreamed that early experience would lead to an incredible connection with the people and cultures of Latin American countries, including their libraries.

It took me more than 20 years, but in 1994 I returned to México—attending the Tri-national Forum /*Foro Trinacional* held on the ITESM campus of Monterrey, México for librarians of Canada, the U.S. and México. Since then, I have made numerous visits to libraries in México and other Latin American countries, from small public libraries to modern university libraries. I have had the marvelous opportunity of providing advocacy training for librarians in México and Latin America, and in the process have learned many important lessons from my colleagues there. The most critical lesson I have learned is how different the library experience is in the United States compared to many Latin American countries. Immigrants from Latin America often come to the U.S. not realizing that there is a full-service public library available to them that provides a wide variety of services for free.

Veronica Myers, a former El Paso Public Library staff member who worked at the Armijo Branch, located very near the U.S.-México border, told me that when she first came to the branch, she would observe dozens of children playing in the park outside the library, while the branch itself would be empty. Her solution? She took the library outside to them, holding storytime and other events in the park. Eventually, she convinced the children—and their families—to come inside to take advantage of the bilingual and Spanish-language resources, as well as the computers with free access to the Internet.

One of the free events held in the park adjoining the Armijo Branch was El Paso's first Día de los Niños / Día de los Libros celebration, which drew 300 children to a *fiesta* that included entertainment, food, storytelling and—most important—free books for all attending. Eight years later that small celebration has now grown into an award-winning, city-wide event raising thousands of dollars to provide entertainment and other attractions for children and families. The main attractions still remain: the event is still free to all who attend, and last year nearly 30,000 children received free books.

El Paso Public Library has served a Spanish-speaking population almost from the day it was established, as the first public library in Texas in 1894. Now that Latinos are becoming a larger economic and cultural force in our nation, many communities are experiencing new and growing Latino populations. This book is intended to help provide information, resources and ideas for serving Latinos, drawing from the experience of libraries in predominantly Latino communities to help inform librarians and library workers across the country.

My earliest experience with providing library service to the Latino community came in the early 1990s while I was working at the Oak Park (IL) Public Library. The Director of the Mexican Fine Arts Center Museum in Chicago lived in my community, and we partnered with him and other area artists to mount several displays and Hispanic Heritage Month celebrations. We also began building our Spanish-language collection, although at that time we had some concerns about how extensive it should be as Oak Park's Latino population made up about 5% of the total population.

That is a question that each community must answer—at what point should the library make a conscious decision to provide collections, programs and services for new or growing populations? There are no easy answers, as library resources are tight in our current economy. My rule of thumb has always been: know your community. Be familiar with your community's changing demographics. Once you observe new populations moving in—particularly if they are already starting to use your library—become familiar with their needs for library services and work with them to fulfill those needs. There are many ways to become familiar with the needs of Latinos in your community, but as Ghada Elturk, Outreach Librarian for the Boulder Public Library, states, "We [librarians] need to get involved in communities rather than surveying them. Our daily involvement is our way to gather information about needs and aspirations."[1]

I quickly realized the wisdom of those words when I moved to the Southwest to serve as the Director of the Thomas Branigan Memorial Library in Las Cruces, New Mexico as well as in my current position at the El Paso Public Library. Serving Latino populations that are close to 70% and 80% respectively has taught me a great deal about building responsive and responsible collections, providing interesting and useful programs, and the importance of marketing libraries to the community.

Librarians have always shared their resources and experience. This book draws heavily on the experience of libraries in predominantly Latino communities to share advice for those who are just beginning to serve Latino populations. Readers will benefit from reading the entire guide, but will also want to use it as a reference tool from time to time. With that in mind, I have drawn what I consider to be the most important "lessons learned"—from both this guide and my own experience.

1. *Know your community* (I cannot stress this enough). As noted above, daily involvement with your community is critical in any situation, but particularly when you are just beginning to serve a particular facet of the community.

   - Assess your community's needs.
   - Conduct focus groups, interviews and surveys.

- Get involved! Join community groups that will allow you to interact with people in your neighborhood.

2. *Take advantage of the many resources* (both human and otherwise) *available to you.*

- Join REFORMA, the National Association to Promote Library and Information Services to Latinos and the Spanish-Speaking. I have been a member for over ten years, and have benefitted enormously from the many resources available from REFORMA—particularly the newsletter and REFORMAnet, an online discussion list.
- Visit the Spanish-language book fairs, such as the Féria Internacional del Libro (FIL) in Guadalajara or other locations. The American Library Association has a wonderful program available to help defray the cost of attending the FIL, held in late November/early December each year.
- Attend the Foro, AMBAC, and other conferences of interest that will bring you in contact with librarians from México and other Latin American countries. Much of what I have learned about the Latino populations I am serving in this country came from my interaction with my generous colleagues across the border.

3. *Learn the language*—it is *the* most important bridge you can build. People in El Paso are constantly surprised when their library director—clearly a *gringa*—can communicate in their language. I have been invited to speak at community meetings conducted primarily in Spanish, and I am interviewed frequently by the Spanish-language media here—which, by the way, is watched and listened to significantly more than the English-language media! There is no better way to get your message out to the community about the library services and programs available.

4. *Recruit library staff—including librarians—from your community.* "Grow your own" librarians if you are not successful in recruiting them from other places. There are many scholarship opportunities

available, such as the American Library Association Spectrum Initiative that provides graduate level library school scholarships for people of color. The library profession still has work to do to reach the diversity levels of the communities we serve. In 2001-2002, 4,119 people received their master's degree in library science—but only 3% of those individuals were Latino.[2]

I have had the opportunity to serve many different communities in the course of my library career, providing me with a lifetime of wonderful memories. Each community had its own unique features—from the fine traditions of the Native American peoples in Muskogee, Oklahoma, to the rich culture and heritage of the African American people I served in Oak Park, Illinois. As librarians, we understand the importance of knowing the individuals we serve, in order to provide the best possible service for them. Our nation's democracy is based on the freedom of information, and our libraries play a vital role in providing information and knowledge for all.

This guide is entitled *¡Bienvenidos! ¡Welcome!* to emphasize the fact that all are welcome in our libraries. I wish you every success as you reach out to the Latino populations in your communities because your outreach will result in an improved quality of life for millions of Americans.

Carol Brey-Casiano
PRESIDENT, AMERICAN LIBRARY ASSOCIATION
& DIRECTOR, EL PASO PUBLIC LIBRARY

¡Bienvenidos!
¡Welcome!

I GREW UP in El Paso, Texas, in a neighborhood shaped by Latino culture and values. This experience has shaped the way I perceive and understand the world. When I went off to college in Atlanta, Georgia and found myself in a predominantly Anglo environment, I had to teach myself to be comfortable within a new cultural context. I had a lot to learn.

Many public libraries are facing shifts in the demographic composition of the communities they serve due to a growing Latino population in their area of service. Public libraries want to serve the Latino population but often don't have the cultural resources or know-how to effectively market their libraries to Latinos. Libraries and librarians will have to step outside of a learned culture and into a culture that may be unfamiliar to them, just like I did when I moved to Atlanta. They may have a lot to learn, but it will be an exciting journey.

This publication is meant as a guide for libraries who would like to increase Latino use of their libraries. This guide offers strategies, ideas and resources for welcoming Latinos into your library community.

The most important ingredient in building Latino participation in your library is willingness. If libraries are to reflect the ideal that a strong democracy and a strong community is built on free access to ideas and information, it is important that libraries actively promote the library and its services to all segments of the community. As a librarian, you cannot assume that everyone in your community knows about the library or feels welcome.

There are five elements to consider when building an effective and comprehensive marketing and outreach strategy whose goal is to actively welcome Latinos to your library. The five elements are addressed as a separate chapter in this guide. These elements are:

- Knowledge
- Responsive Collections
- Library Services and Programming

- Outreach and Publicity
- Access

In moving forward, it is important to build on your strengths in each of these areas and identify and develop an action plan around any weaknesses or gaps in service.

In building an action plan that addresses each of these elements, this guide will help you to:

1. Build a base of knowledge about the Latino community in your service area to inform your marketing strategy and to assure that your strategy is a reflection of the needs and interests in the Latino community.
2. Develop a collection of books, magazines, videos, audiotapes and resources that meet the specific demand created by your local Latino community.
3. Develop programs, activities and services that are of interest to the Latinos in your service area.
4. Generate excitement and interest about your library, services, programs and activities in the Latino community.
5. Provide comfortable and easy access to the library for the local Latino community.

Our libraries and our communities are made stronger when we actively reach out to new library users and allow these library users to influence and change the way we think about our libraries. Remember that good will, a fearless heart and a willingness to listen are critical to building a patron base that feels welcome in your library and in your community. You will be successful because you are willing to change and grow to respond to new needs in your community.

Chapter One

KNOWLEDGE

Build a base of knowledge about the Latino community in your service area to inform your marketing strategy and to assure that your strategy is a reflection of the needs and interests in the Latino community.

THE LATINO population in the United States is not homogeneous. The words "Latino" and "Hispanic" are broad catchall terms generally referencing that a person is descended from a country in Latin America or Spain, a country where Spanish is the main language. The words Latino and Hispanic are often used interchangeably, but it is important to remember that shared language does not mean shared behavior, shared values, shared experience or shared perceptions. An effective marketing strategy should reflect a knowledge and understanding of the diversity within the Latino community in your area and should acknowledge and respect the individuality of all library users.

It is important to learn as much as possible about the Latino community in your service area before making investments in collections, programming, services, publicity and staffing. Not knowing the specifics of your service area or generalizing your outreach strategy to a broad conception of what you think Latino is can be counterproductive and costly. This is especially true if you assume some of the common misconceptions about Latinos.

DEMOGRAPHICS

Much has been made in the media and in civic dialogue about how the growing Latino population is quickly changing the demographic landscape of the United States. It is important to understand what is happening nationally as a context for understanding your own local community.

Size. Latinos today represent nearly 13.3% of the U.S. population, 37.4 million nationwide.[1] They are the largest minority group in the United States. Christy Haubegger—president and publisher of *Latina Magazine*, the first glossy national magazine for Latinas—has pointed out that the

Latino population in the United States is larger than the population of Canada—you don't hear anybody calling Canada a "niche market" as the Latino market in the United States is so often referred to. Undoubtedly, Latinos represent an important economic, political and cultural force in the United States with more than one in eight people in the United States reporting that they are of Latino origin.

Country of Origin and Identity. Latinos in the United States are a culturally, demographically and geographically diverse population. The largest Latino population group in the United States is persons of Mexican origin (66.9% of the total Latino population), followed by Puerto Rican (8.6%) and then Cuban-Americans (3.7%). Central and South Americans represent 14.3% of the Latino population in the United States.[2] Latinos come from as many as 20 different countries, and some of these countries share very little in common other than the Spanish language.

Hispanics by origin: 2002

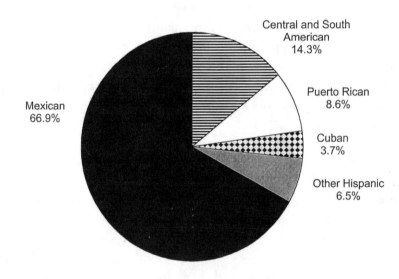

Source: U.S. Census Bureau, Annual Demographic Supplement to the March 2002 Current Population Survey

In 2000, the first generation of foreign-born Latinos represented 40% of the Latino population, while the second generation represented 28%. The third plus generation made up 32% of the Latino population. "As it continues to grow, the composition of the Latino population is undergoing a fundamental change: Births in the United States are outpacing immigration as the key source of growth. Over the next twenty years this will produce an important shift in the makeup of the Latino population with second-generation Latinos—the U.S.-born children of immigrants—emerging as the largest component of that population."[3]

Identity and ties to the country of origin are often determined by how long a Latino and his or her family has lived in the United States. A large number of Latinos (88%) say that they identify themselves in terms of their country of origin (for example as a Mexicano or a Puerto Rican). However, foreign-born Latinos are more likely than native-born Latinos (95% vs. 74%), and second-generation Latinos are more likely than third-generation Latinos (82% vs. 66%) to say they use their country of origin to identify themselves.[4]

As with all words that we use to identify who we are, the language that Latinos use to identify themselves is expressive of complicated political, historical, geographic and linguistic understanding of a group in relation to other groups. For example, when I asked a young Latina I know who also grew up in El Paso what word she uses to describe herself, she said, "I don't call myself Chicana. That's too political. Not Mexican-American either. That's not political enough. Not Latina or Hispanic. Those words are too Census Bureau. Not Mexicana. That denies that I am also American. No, I call myself a *fronteriza* (directly translated as a woman from the Border). I belong to the Border."

Because of modern forms of communication (Internet, telephone, widespread Spanish-language media in the United States) and geographic proximity, present day immigration is extremely different from earlier trends in immigration. Marketers and social scientists, who were expecting Latinos to assimilate to the culture of the United States in the same way as European immigrants, have been very surprised. "Immigrants today are more likely to be at once 'here' and 'there,' articulating dual consciousness and dual identities and, in the process, bridging increasingly unbounded national spaces,"[5] writes Harvard professor Marcelo Suárez-Orozco in his article titled "Everything You Ever Wanted to Know About Assimilation but Were Afraid to Ask." Acculturation has become a much more dynamic and unpredictable process with many Latinos adopting the values and attitudes of the United States while at the same time retaining aspects of their culture from their country of origin.

Language. A clear example of a decidedly different acculturation process in Latino communities than in other immigrant communities is the continued prevalence of Spanish-language use among Latinos. "Although two-thirds of Latinos living in the U.S. were born here, 59% of those surveyed by the Strategy Research said Spanish was the first language they learned to speak. Most immigrants to the U.S. retain Spanish even if they also learn English, and many families insist that Spanish be spoken at home."[6]

The United States is the second most populous Spanish-speaking nation in the world, after México. In Pat Mora's children's book, *The Rainbow Tulip*, the narrator says, "My brothers and I speak English outside the house and Spanish inside the house. My father says, '*Hija*, this house is a piece of México.'"[7] This is a common experience for many Latinos whose parents want them to be able to communicate in English but who want the intimate language of home to be tied to their roots and their culture.

Many second- and third-generation Latinos who did not grow up knowing Spanish are now learning the language to reconnect to their heritage. In communities where Spanish use is prevalent, many non-Latinos know Spanish or want to learn Spanish.

There are generation differences in Spanish- and/or English-language use among Latinos—39% of the first generation speak almost entirely in Spanish, 28% of the second generation speak Spanish at home and English elsewhere and 33% of the third and beyond generations speak English as their primary language. Even though many Latinos maintain the Spanish language as a way of expressing their culture, about 9 in 10 Latinos (89%) indicate that they believe immigrants need to learn to speak English to succeed in the United States.[8]

Small Businesses. According to the 1997 Economic Census, the number of Latino-owned businesses grew at a faster pace than any other class of business. Latinos owned almost 1.2 million of all U.S. businesses in 1997, employing over 1.3 million persons and generating $186.3 billion in business revenues. In 1997, Latino-owned firms accounted for 5.8% of the 20.8 million businesses in the United States, 1.3% of their employment and 1.0% of their receipts.[9]

Educational Attainment. Educational attainment rates for Latinos lag behind non-Latino Whites. Sixteen percent of Latinos do not have a high school diploma and 27% have less than a 9th grade education, compared to 7% and 4% for non-Latino Whites. Also, Latinos are less likely than non-Latino Whites to have a bachelor's degree or another form of advanced degree.[10] Educational attainment is a huge concern in Latino communities, and they often turn to the libraries for support in achieving educational attainment goals.

Hispanic Educational Attainment
(As percent of each population 25 years or older)

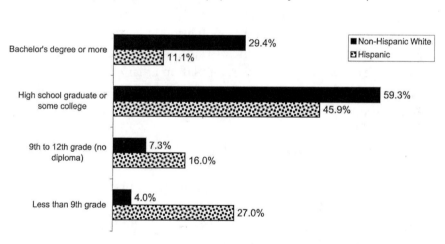

Source: U.S. Census Bureau, Annual Demographic Supplement to the March 2002 Current Population Survey

Online. The comScore Media Matrix published in June 2003 indicates that there are 12.5 million Latinos online. A little less than half of these online users prefer Spanish. Latino consumers are spending an hour more online each week (9.5 hours per week at home) than the average non-Latino consumer.[11] The Internet is valued as an important source of information for Latinos: 75% of Latinos surveyed for a UCLA Internet Project indicated that the Internet was either "extremely important" or "very important" as a source of information for them, compared to only 60% of non-Latinos surveyed.[12]

In building a base of knowledge about the Latino community in your area, start off with a general demographic profile. This preliminary data will give you a foundation on which to build a fuller picture of how to best serve the Latino community. The American Factfinder on the Census Bureau's website (www.census.gov) is a good tool for building such a snapshot. Some questions to answer in putting together this demographic profile will include:

- How many Latinos live in your library's service area?
- What is the population of Latinos in various age groups (under 5 years, 18 years and over, 65 years and over)?
- What is the educational attainment of Latinos in the area? How does this compare to the population at large?
- What is the per capita income of Latinos in the service area? How does this compare to the population at large?
- What is the language spoken at home? For Latinos who speak Spanish in the home, how many report speaking English "not well"?
- What are the countries of origin of Latinos living in your community?
- What percentage of the Latino community is first generation or "foreign born"? Of those Latinos who are first generation, what is their citizenship status? What percentage of the Latino community are second or third generation?

Community Assessment

Once you have developed a broad demographic picture, you will want to refine that information to find specific information about Latinos in your community. What do they want from your library? How you can make your library more welcoming to Latinos in your community? How is your library perceived in the Latino community? This information will help you develop your marketing and outreach strategy. Also, if you are unfamiliar with the Latino community, this process will help you to build cultural competence and know-how, and it will help you build important relationships with the Latino community.

Some important questions to ask about your local Latino community are:

- Are ties to the country of origin strong and important to the community?
- What expectations do Latinos have of the library?
- What is their perception of the library and the services that the library provides?
- What has been the experience of Latinos in your community with your library?
- For first-generation Latinos, what was their experience of libraries in their home country? How are those experiences different than the tradition of the library in the United States?
- Are there obstacles that prevent Latinos from using the library? Obstacles might include long distances between Latino neighborhoods and branch libraries, lack of information about library services; or institutional distrust as a result of racism or ethnic conflict in the community.
- What are important holidays, cultural events and traditions? How are they celebrated or observed?
- What are the community's book reading interests—literature, politics, poetry, how-to, romance?
- What reference titles, magazines, videos, audiotapes and resources would be of interest to this target audience?
- What are the local concerns of Latinos (e.g., building small businesses, education, building leadership), and what resources can the library provide to help address these concerns?
- What kind of programs would be of interest in this community?
- Would this community rather read in Spanish or English or both?
- Would they appreciate having the choice of being able to read in either Spanish or English?
- What media venues are most effective in reaching this target population?

- What word-of-mouth networks are most responsible for spreading information in the Latino community?
- Where do Latinos gather and share information in the community (churches, community centers, parks, schools, grocery stores, laundromats)?
- Who are the community leaders and connectors who can help build a bridge between the library and the Latino community? Community connectors are people who—by virtue of their personality or by virtue of the work that they do—know and communicate with lots of people on a regular basis.

There are several ways that you can gather information that will inform your marketing strategy. These include interviews, surveys and questionnaires and advisory councils. These gathering processes have the added benefit of serving as a form of marketing. When you actively engage in an information-gathering effort geared at learning more about the Latino community, Latinos know that the library is interested in serving the Latino community and that you wants ideas and information about how best to do this. Regardless of how you choose to gather information, it is important to make sure that you always start by talking about the library and what the library's goals are in soliciting information.

As Ghada Elturk, the Outreach Librarian at the Boulder Public Library, points out, the most successful efforts go beyond a limited information-gathering process. "We [librarians] need to get involved in communities rather than surveying them. Our daily involvement is our way to gather information about needs and aspirations."[13]

Interviews. Informal interviews with teachers, community leaders, neighborhood peer leaders, business leaders, church leaders, school leaders, community center directors and others who are an active part of the Latino community are a great way to find out what is going on in a community and to gather support for your efforts. Interviews should be in person rather than over the phone so that you can build a friendly, face-to-face relationship with the person you are interviewing. In addition to asking for information, ask the people you interview to help you connect the library to the Latino community.

As you begin identifying the leaders and the connectors in the Latino community, build a database of people and organizations that can help you disseminate information about the library, continue to keep you informed about the needs and interests in the Latino community and can be counted on for input when you have questions or ideas. Keep these people informed of your efforts on an ongoing basis.

Surveys and Questionnaires. Surveys are a good way to quantify and prioritize information provided by a large segment of a target market. If you choose to survey as a means for gathering information, decide what information you need and how you will use and analyze the information before designing the survey.

In designing the survey, use clear and precise language. If you have determined from your demographic profile that a large portion of your target market speaks Spanish, create a bilingual survey. Keep your questions brief and your survey short. Start with general questions and end with more specific questions.

For the most part, questions should have prescribed answers such as YES/NO, AGREE/DISAGREE or a series of options including OTHER. For example, "I use the library a) once a week, b) once a month, c) rarely or d) not at all." Structuring questions and answers this way will make it easy for you to tabulate and analyze the results of the survey.

Always provide ample white space for respondents to provide more detailed responses. Some great nuggets of truth and useful ideas will find their way onto the survey if you give people enough room to share.

It is important to implement the survey process so that you get a high rate of response. Include a brief introduction about why the survey is important to making the library more welcoming to Latinos. Make it convenient for people to fill out the survey. If you mail the survey, include a self-addressed stamped envelope. Follow up to remind people why the survey is important. Ask people to fill out surveys at schools or community fairs where the one-on-one interaction will influence their decision to fill out the survey. Provide an incentive that will make a potential respondent more likely to fill out the survey.

Advisory Council. Another option for gathering information is to form a group of advisors. This council should be made up of community leaders and connectors in the Latino community. Often the best advisors are active and gregarious individuals who like to talk and share information with others. These individuals may not have formal connections or titles, but they are people who everyone knows and counts on for information.

Initially, an advisory council can help provide you with a framework of information and contacts to get you started. More importantly, this group can help you as you begin to implement your marketing strategy. If convened regularly, an advisory council can provide feedback from the community, provide ideas and resources for ongoing efforts, serve as a place for you to brainstorm about what will work and won't work and continually connect the library to the Latino community.

•

Remember that information gathering is an ongoing process and that your marketing strategy should be fluid enough to respond to new information, new ideas and new sources of information. Because information gathering is also a form of marketing and a way to welcome people into an institution, the library should continue to solicit information and be open to new ideas. The marketing message implied by a visible, easy-to-use "Suggestions welcome / *Acceptamos sugerencias*" box is that the library user is a valuable part of the library community. This message should not only be a visual message, but also a message communicated by the way that the library staff interacts and responds to library users' ideas and suggestions.

Share the information that you have gathered with your library staff and with community advisors. Use this information to shape your library's efforts to effectively market the library to the Latino community. Evaluate the information to assess whether your current collection, services, programming and outreach adequately respond to needs in the Latino community. Where gaps exist, prioritize areas for action. Identify library staff and community volunteers and partners who will be critical in implementing an effective strategy. Include these people in the decision-making process. Identify resources that you will need to act effectively. Identify achievable goals and a standard for measuring success. Identify timelines for action. And most importantly, act.

As you begin this process, it is important to know that there are many resources and organizations available to help you effectively market your library to Latinos. You are not alone. One of the most valuable resources available to librarians working with Latinos is REFORMA, the National Association to Promote Library Services to Latinos and the Spanish-Speaking. José Ruiz-Álvarez, the 2004-2005 President of REFORMA, said that for him the most important part of being a member of REFORMA "is the powerful networking possibilities one has through membership in REFORMA. There are numerous professionals in this country who are working very hard to find innovative ways to serve Latino populations in libraries, and REFORMA has been a very powerful resource-sharing vehicle for those looking for ideas, support and inspiration."

REFORMA's mission is to:
- actively promote the development of library collections to include Spanish-language and Latino-oriented materials;
- recruit more bilingual and bicultural library professionals and support staff;
- develop library services and programs that meet the needs of the Latino community;
- establish a national information and support network among individuals who share our goals;
- educate the U.S. Latino population in regards to the availability and types of library services; and
- lobby to preserve existing library resource centers serving the interests of Latinos.

REFORMA has an information-packed website with links to useful resources and ideas. REFORMA members receive the REFORMA newsletter and have access to the REFORMAnet discussion list. REFORMAnet is a vehicle for members to share ideas and information and ask questions about serving Latinos and Spanish speakers. Members can also join one of the twenty local chapters of REFORMA that have been formed to act on local issues. REFORMA has a formal mentoring program to match seasoned REFORMA librarians with librarians who will benefit from this experience and guidance.

RESOURCES

**REFORMA, National Association to Promote Library Services
to Latinos and the Spanish-Speaking**
    Contact: Sandra Rios Balderrama
    Address: P.O. Box 25963, Scottsdale, AZ 85255-0116
    Phone: 480-471-7452   *Fax:* 480-471-7442
    Website: www.reforma.org
    Email: REFORMAoffice@riosbalderrama.com

PLUS (Public Libraries Using Spanish)
Description: PLUS is a searchable resource bank of useful material in Spanish
and ideas for public libraries serving Spanish speakers.
    Website: www.sol-plus.net/plus/home.htm

Chapter 2

RESPONSIVE COLLECTIONS

Develop a collection of books, magazines, videos, audiotapes and resources that meet the specific demand created by your local Latino community.

LATINOS' interests in books and other library resources, like any other group of people, are broad and based on individual tastes and community values. Latinos place a high value on being able to maintain their customs, language and culture. Because of this, Latinos are drawn to books and resources that are culturally relevant, that speak to their experience as Latinos in the United States, and that are by Latinos or by writers from their country of origin.

Part of building a responsive collection is to act on ideas and suggestions from the community. Ghada Elturk, the Outreach Librarian at Boulder Public Library, asks volunteers from a particular target market to help her with collection development. She asks volunteers to take catalogs out into the community to see what people would be the most interested in seeing in the library. Once the books are purchased, she asks volunteers to read the books and summarize the content in English to help in cataloging the books. "For people to see their suggestions taken seriously, and see their selections on the shelves, was a major event. They flocked to the library with family and friends."[1] Formalizing a process for people to make suggestions about what kinds of books that they want to see in the library helps create a feeling of ownership of the library.

SPANISH-LANGUAGE BOOKS AND BOOKS BY LATINOS

The Spanish language represents an important way of transmitting culture in the Latino community. This means that Spanish-language books and bilingual books could be an important part of bringing Latinos into your library if many of the Latinos in your service area speak Spanish. Again, it is important to survey and know the needs of the community in your service area before making these kinds of assumptions and investments. And though Latinos might be interested in the latest Tom Clancy novel in translation, they will also be interested in original works in Spanish and books in Spanish that relate to their experience as Latinos in the United States.

An important thing to note is that not only Latinos will be interested in these types of books. In communities with large and growing Latino populations, non-Latinos who have grown up with Latinos will also be interested in these types of books and resources. As the Latino culture grows not only in size but also in influence, non-Latinos are increasingly interested in Latino culture and in learning Spanish.

English-language titles written by Latinos should be an important part of your collection when serving the Latino community. Classic titles and books by emerging Latino voices in all different genres should be considered and included.

Loida Garcia-Febo is the Spanish Language Collections Manager at Queens Library in Jamaica, New York, which has the largest circulation of Spanish-language titles in the nation. Garcia-Febo works to maintain a balance in the book collection between original works in Spanish and books in translation. She also tries to include both Spanish classics and contemporary and original works from Latin American writers and Latino writers. The main draw in her collection is original works in original Spanish from Latin American writers. She works diligently to make sure that the collection reflects the demographics of the communities. If she finds that a particular service area is growing to include more Columbians, for example, she will include books by Columbian authors in her collection.

Garcia-Febo says that contemporary music and movies from Latin America are very popular. Queens Library users usually are looking for original movies in Spanish, rather than popular American movies with Spanish subtitles. She says new releases as well as old movie classics are equally as popular.

Because this segment of the market is still in its infancy, Garcia-Febo has found that responsive collection development means a constant dialogue with distributors, publishers and users. This team approach to collection development keeps her abreast of what's new and what users want. It also keeps distributors informed about what is working and what is not working in the libraries. If library users are asking for biographies of prominent Latin American political leaders, she will call distributors to find out what they have available. If nothing has been published or is available through the distributors, she will call publishers she knows to let them know that she is seeing more demand for these particular types of titles. A listing of Spanish-language distributors and publishers can be found at the end of this guide.

Garcia-Febo recommends that librarians in the Spanish-language marketplace test a small collection to see what works and what doesn't work before making any major resource allocations. Queens Library keeps a rotating collection of tried-and-true titles on hand. If a branch manager sees that they are getting more requests for Spanish-language titles or if there are demographic shifts to include more Latinos in a particular area, branch managers can request a rotating collection to try for six months. Special attention is paid to the circulation of the rotating collection to see what works. Future decisions are based on what is working and on the feedback from branch managers and library users.

Where Spanish-language collections should be shelved is often a point of debate among librarians. Some librarians argue that Spanish-language materials should be integrated into the larger collection so as not to treat Spanish-language users as a separate class of library users. Others argue that providing a separate section in the library dedicated to Spanish-language materials makes accessing those materials much easier for library users. Asking library users for their input on where to shelf Spanish-language materials will help you to make the best decision for your community. You will want to balance ease-of-access with providing a comfortable, non-threatening library environment in making a decision about where to place Spanish-language material.

RESOURCES

Críticas, An English Speaker's Guide to the Latest Spanish Language Titles
Description: Críticas is a comprehensive review of the latest in Spanish-language publishing written in English. *Críticas* is an authoritative one-stop source for English-language reviews of new adult and children's titles from the international Spanish-language publishing world. *Críticas* also covers Spanish-language publishing news as it pertains to U.S. readers, librarians and booksellers.

For English-language titles that have been translated into Spanish and for bilingual books, *Críticas* also provides a review of the translation as well as a review of the content. Not all translations are created equally—an accurate and high-quality translation will be important to your Spanish-speaking library users.

Críticas' website also has valuable information including "The Basics: 100 Fiction Titles You Should Stock" and a monthly listing of *Críticas'* bestsellers.

One of the most valuable tools on the *Críticas'* website is a comprehensive directory of everything anyone would ever want to know about the Spanish-Language Publishing Marketplace. There is a listing with contact information of distributors, wholesalers and book, audio and video publishers.

Críticas is distributed as a monthly e-newsletter with two special print supplements.

Website: www.criticasmagazine.com

Guadalajara International Book Fair / Féria Internacional del Libro (FIL)
Description: For librarians who want to build their Spanish-language collection, the Guadalajara International Book Fair (FIL) is a must. Everyone who publishes in Latin America is there. The FIL is a book fair hosted by Guadalajara, México in the fall of each year. It is the largest Spanish-language book event in the world. The FIL offers firsthand access to the latest publications in Spanish; an exhibit of more than 75,000 titles; access to the complete catalogs of more than 900 publishers from over 25 countries; networking opportunities with 8,000 book professionals; literary programming with Latin American authors and lectures on Mexican culture.

The American Library Association and the FIL have partnered to provide FREE PASSES (including the costs of airfare, hotel accommodations and registration) to 150 ALA librarians who work in the area of Spanish-language acquisitions and/or are working to build their Spanish-language collection to better serve their community and users.

FIL Website: www.fil.com.mx (a tab at the bottom of the page will take you to an English translation of the site)
For more information about the FIL and the ALA-FIL FREE PASS program:
Contact: David Unger
Address: FIL New York, Division of Humanities NAC 5/225
The City College of New York, New York, NY 10031
Phone: 212-650-7925   *Fax:* 212-650-7912
E-mail: FILNY@aol.com

LIBROS EN VENTA en América Latina y España (Spanish-Language Books In and Out of Print)
Description: Available in an online format or on CD-ROM, *LIBROS EN VEN-TA en América Latina y España* (LEV) is a reference source for Spanish-language books-in-print. LIBROS EN VENTA includes in-print titles from over 26,000 Latin American and Spanish publishers. LEV covers all types of books, including: adult fiction, non-fiction, juvenile, scholarly subjects, textbooks, reprints, legal, medical, business, science & technology, religious and more. LEV's

publisher information includes publisher street addresses, phone numbers, fax numbers, e-mail addresses, web URLs and the names of any distributors and sales outlets.

Publisher: National Information Services Corporation, NISC USA
Address: Wyman Towers, 3100 St. Paul Street, Baltimore, MD 21218
Phone: 410-243-0797   *Fax:* 410-243-0982
Email: sales@nisc.com
Website: www.nisc.com/factsheets/qlev.asp

EMIERT: Ethnic and Multicultural Information Exchange Round Table

Description: EMIERT's purpose is to "serve as a source of information on recommended ethnic collections, services, and programs; to organize task forces, institutes, and workshops to carry out the functions of the Round Table as defined in the petition; to develop for Annual conferences forums and symposia programs that deal with the key issues of ethnicity and librarianship; and to maintain a liaison with the Office of Library Outreach Services and cooperate with other ALA units, including the caucuses in joint projects for the betterment of outreach services."

Website: http://www.ala.org/ala/emiert/aboutemiert/aboutemiert.htm

BOOK AWARDS

Juan Rulfo Award to the Latin American and Caribbean Literature

Description: This award extols the quality and importance of contemporary literature written in any of the languages spoken in Latin America, the Caribbean and the Iberian Peninsula. This honor is awarded annually at the FIL.

Website: www.fil.com.mx

Latino Book Awards

Description: Latino Literacy Now created these awards, in recognition of the many positive contributions being made to the world of Latino literature by publishers and writers. Awards are presented each year in seven categories: Children & Young Adult, Nonfiction-English, Nonfiction-Spanish or Bilingual, Fiction-English, Fiction-Spanish, Design and Best First Book.

Sponsor Organization: Latino Literacy Now
Address: 2777 Jefferson St. Ste 200, Carlsbad, CA 92008
Phone: 760-434-4484   *Fax:* 760-434-7476
Website: www.lbff.us/sponsors/press-room/latinobook/index.htm

Premio Atzlán, Literary Prize

Description: Premio Atzlán is a national literary prize established by Rudolfo and Pat Anaya in 1993 to honor a book of fiction by an emerging Chicana or Chicano writer.

Sponsor Organization: General Library, Dean's Office
MSC05 3020, 1 University of New México, Albuquerque, NM 87131-1466
Contact: Teresa Marquez at 505-277-0582 / tmarquez@unm.edu
or Dina Ma'ayan, at 505-277-7197 / dinam@unm.edu

Sor Juana Inés de la Cruz Award

Description: This award is given for an outstanding book of fiction by a Latin American woman. The honor is awarded annually at the FIL.
Website: www.fil.com.mx

CHILDREN'S BOOKS

In the Latino culture, a premium is placed on education, on children attaining more and doing better than the generation before. Because of this, visiting the library is often a family event with Latinos interested in children's books that are culturally relevant and in Spanish-language children's books. All children love to see their own experiences and language and perceptions reflected in books. Igniting a children's love for literature often means finding that one book that speaks directly to a child's sense of self in relationship to the world.

There are two formats that are used by publishers for Spanish-language children's titles. Some publishers produce bilingual editions, in which Spanish and English share the same page. Bilingual books, especially those with repetitive language, are great for learning a second language. Bilingual books are also a cost-effective option for providing content in both Spanish and English. Some companies publish dual editions of a single title, one in Spanish and the other in English. Within the publishing world and academia, there is often debate about what Spanish-language formats work best for children acquiring a second language. What is often lost in the debate and what is the most important question to answer in choosing books for your collection is, "Will this book ignite a child's love for literature?"

RESOURCES

Barahona Center for the Study of Books in Spanish for Children and Adolescents
Description: The Center serves as an information center on books about Latino people and culture and about books in Spanish and their value in the education of English-speaking and Spanish-speaking children and adolescents. The Center has a searchable online database of recommended books in Spanish and recommended books in English about Latinos.

> *Address:* California State University San Marcos
> Kellogg Library, 5th Floor, 333 S Twin Oaks Valley Road
> San Marcos, California 92096-0001
> *Phone:* 760-750-4070   *Fax:* 760-750-4073
> *E-Mail:* ischon@csusm.edu
> *Website:* www.csusm.edu/csb

REFERENCE TITLES

Bilingual Children's Books in English and Spanish / Los Libros Bilingües para niños en Inglés y en Español; An Annotated Bibliography, 1942 through 2001 bilingual edition / Una Bibliografía con Anotaciones, 1942 a 2001 edición bilingüe. By Doris Cruger Dale. McFarland and Company, Inc. (www.mcfarlandpub.com), 2003. ISBN 0-7864-1316-6
Description: This bibliography lists more than 400 bilingual children's titles— mostly picture books, with alphabet and counting books also included—that feature text in both Spanish and English in the same volume. Annotations to the entries provide a summary of each book's contents, along with information on awards the book has received and a list of reviews gathered from *Children's Book Review Index*. This bilingual edition includes introduction, table of contents and subject indexing in both English and Spanish.

Children's and Young Adult Literature by Latino Writers: A Guide for Librarians, Teachers, Parents and Students. By Sherry York.
Linworth Publishing (www.linworth.com), 2002. ISBN 1-58683-062-7
Description: This title's easy-to-use format provides access to the sometimes difficult-to-find resources for young people written by Latino authors. The author has included complete bibliographic information for a variety of titles in various genres including novels, chapter books, short stories, folklore, drama, poetry and nonfiction. A list of additional resource materials, as well as publisher information and an index, is also included. For each book, complete bibliographic information is included, as well as a list of editions, a summary, interest and

reading levels, test availability in Accelerated Reader and Reading Counts, awards and a list of reviews.

The Best of the Latino Heritage: A Guide to the Best Juvenile Books about Latino People and Cultures. By Isabel Schon. Scarecrow Press (www.scarecrowpress.com), 1996. ISBN 0-8108-3221-6
Description: This guide was designed to help teachers and librarians identify books that will provide kindergarten through high school students with an understanding of the cultures of Latino people. Books are listed by country and include complete bibliographic information as well as a summary of content, annotations regarding the strengths and weaknesses of the work and notes on grade level appropriateness. The guide includes an author index, title index and subject index.

BOOK AWARDS

Américas Award
Description: The Américas Award is given in recognition of U.S. works of fiction, poetry, folklore or selected non-fiction (from picture books to works for young adults) published in the previous year in English or Spanish that authentically and engagingly portray Latin America, the Caribbean or Latinos in the United States. The award is sponsored by the national Consortium of Latin American Studies Programs (CLASP).

> *Contact:* Julie Kline, Award Coordinator
> *Address:* Latin American & Caribbean Studies, UW-Milwaukee
> Pearse 168, 2513 E. Hartford Ave., Milwaukee, WI 53211
> *Phone:* 414-229-5986   *Fax:* 414-229-2879   *Email:* jkline@uwm.edu
> *Website:* www.uwm.edu/Dept/CLACS/outreach/americas.html

Pura Belpré Award
Description: Established in 1996, the Pura Belpré Award is presented to a Latino or Latina writer and illustrator whose work best portrays, affirms and celebrates the Latino cultural experience in an outstanding work of literature for children and youth. It is co-sponsored by the Association of Library Service to Children and REFORMA.

> *Websites:* www.reforma.org/belpreawardGeneric.html
> www.ala.org/alsc/belpre.html

Tomás Rivera Mexican American Children's Book Award

Description: The award was established in 1995 by Southwest Texas State University to encourage authors, illustrators and publishers of books that authentically reflect the lives of Mexican-American children and young adults in the Southwestern region of the United States.

Address: Texas State University–San Marcos College of Education
2001 Education Building, 601 University
San Marcos, Texas 78666
Phone: 512-245-2044   *Fax:* 512-245-7911
Email: JL08@txstate.edu
Website: www.education.txstate.edu/subpages/tomasrivera

Chapter 3

Library Services and Programming

Develop programs, activities and services that are of interest to the Latinos in your service area.

PROVIDING services and programs that are relevant and of interest to Latinos in your service area is a great way to connect your library to the Latino community. In developing services and programming, pay attention to your target market to make sure that the program or service will be accessible, useful and interesting. For example, if your program is aimed at families, make sure that you schedule the event or service when parents and children are available for family time. If your target market is predominantly Spanish-speaking, give the event a bilingual title and make sure that the event is coordinated and hosted by Spanish-speaking librarians or volunteers.

If this program or service represents some of your first efforts at bringing Latinos into the library or if you have identified trust as one of the obstacles that prevents Latinos from using your library, plan the program offsite at a place in the community where Latinos feel comfortable and at home (schools, churches, community centers, fiestas, community fairs). Another option is to coordinate the program with community partners who are a part of the Latino community or are trusted in the Latino community.

This kind of introductory programming will allow the library staff to build familiarity and establish trust within the Latino community. Face-to-face personal contact with friendly, helpful and personable library staff is the best way to market your library in the community.

Introduction to the Library

Never make assumptions about what people do or don't know about the library. The public library tradition in the United States is different from the public library tradition in Latin America. Immigrants to the United States may not know that libraries loan books out free of charge or that public libraries can be used by anyone in the community. If you have identified knowledge of library services as one of the obstacles to accessing and using the library, you will want to spend some time educating your target market about what the library offers and how to use it.

Introductions to the library could include tours of the library and individualized training on how to access the catalog of library materials. If your target market is predominantly Spanish-speaking, provide tours and training in Spanish or in an inclusive bilingual format. If no one on your staff is Spanish-speaking, ask volunteers to help. PLUS: Public Libraries Using Spanish (www.sol-plus.net) recommends that you not shy away from leading a tour (*orientación* in Spanish) if language is an obstacle. "Your limited or absent Spanish can be an advantage if you remember that libraries exist not to be explained, but *explored*."[1]

Consider organizing a library tour as a treasure hunt. Using the following list, cut out each item and distribute them among your visitors. Send visitors out to find the items and then bring them back to discuss where the items were found.

PLUS Library Treasure Hunt[2]

ITEM IN SPANISH	ITEM IN ENGLISH
Una película en español	A Spanish-language film
Un diccionario español-inglés	A Spanish-English dictionary
Un periódico local	A local newspaper
Un recetario	A cookbook
Un video para niños	A video for children
Una revista en español	A Spanish-language magazine
Formas para pagar impuestos	Tax forms
Algo que se trata de computadoras	Something about computers
Un libro duradero para niños	A board book for children
Música latina en CD	Latin music on CD
Recursos para el aprendizaje del inglés	English-study resources
Un manual de reparación de carros	An auto-repair manual
Algo sobre su país	Something about your country
Un folleto con el horario de camiones	A bus schedule
Un libro de consulta	A reference book
que no sale de la biblioteca	that doesn't leave the library

If you are using programming as an introduction to the library, make sure to include information about the library as part of the event. In your introduction and conclusion to the program, invite attendees to tour the library. Include library tours as part of the program. Provide library card applications and library information at the site of the event. Stress that library services and library use are free (*gratis* in Spanish) and available to everyone.

Programming and Services for Children

Storytime. Storytime is an age-old, cost-effective way to connect children and families to libraries, to literacy and to a love of literature. When using storytime as a way to reach out to Latino children and families, consider taking storytime out of the library and on the road. Share stories at local malls, at day cares and at schools. Then tie storytime back to the library. Talk to children about the library and sign them up for library cards.

If your target market is predominantly Spanish-speaking or bilingual, provide a Spanish storytime or a bilingual storytime. If no one on your staff is fluent in Spanish, ask community leaders, teachers, actors or story-tellers to share stories with children in Spanish

Sharing a story in a bilingual format is a great way to bring together children who speak different languages in an inclusive and comfortable environment. Reading a story in a bilingual format increases a children's comprehension of a second language, as well as teaches the patterns and rhythms of a second language. It also increases a child's confidence in their ability to understand and enjoy a second language.

There are a couple of ways to share stories in a bilingual format. Two presenters can read a story, sharing a short section or page of the story in one language and then reading the same section or page in the second language. The book can be in a bilingual format or in a dual edition. Each presenter can hold up a copy of the book while reading back and forth between Spanish and English.

Another way to read a story in a bilingual format is to mix the two languages together, reading the story in a children's first language and enriching it with the second language. The best stories to read or tell in this format are highly repetitive stories with a predictable structure. Initially, read the "framework" of the story in the children's first language.

When the main characters are introduced, you can name them in both the first and second language and then begin to replace the names with the second language as the story progresses. Also, when there are repetitive phrases and language in the story, the phrases or language can be read in the first language and then repeated in the second language. As the children get more familiar with the story, work in the second language wherever it will fit smoothly.

Bilingual storyteller Joe Hayes says that when he tells stories bilingually, "the greatest delight for Spanish speakers comes from my saying things in Spanish first and then translating them to English. So often the children whose first language is Spanish are struggling to understand things that come so easily to English speakers. This style of telling gives the Spanish speakers an advantage for a change, and they even have the extra satisfaction of their English-only friends turning to them and asking, 'What's he saying?'"[3]

When selecting books for storytime, pick titles that are meaningful to Latinos, that reflect their experience of the world or where the children can see people like them reflected in the story and the illustrations. Books that retell stories from the Latino cultural tradition are popular storytime hits. For example, the story of the weeping woman *la Llorona* or the bogeyman e*l Cucuy* are popular stories in Latin American and in Latino communities throughout the United States. There are many books that share different retellings of *la Llorona* and *el Cucuy*. These stories offer an opportunity for the children listening to share their own family version of the story.

Storytime programming can be enhanced with crafts, songs, rhymes, puppet shows, plays and food. Ask volunteers or parents to share crafts, rhymes or songs that they learned growing up.

Día de los Niños / Día de los Libros.
Día de los Niño (Day of the Child) is a popular celebration of children in México. This day recognizes children, pays homage to their importance in society and endorses their well being. Pat Mora, a popular author and an advocate for children's literacy, teamed up with REFORMA, the National Association of Bilingual Educators and MANA, a National Latina Organization to celebrate children and literacy in a nationwide event known as Día de los Niños / Día de los Libros.

Celebrated on April 30 each year, libraries across the country have built the event into a premiere children's event that everyone in the community looks forward to celebrating. Each local event takes on a character of its own and can include book giveaways, crafts, music, dance, author visits, storytelling, writing workshops, food and outdoor activities. Regardless of how the event is celebrated, the key concept is celebrating children, culture, literature and literacy.

El Paso started their celebration in 1997 at a local branch library. Expecting 50 children to arrive, they were overwhelmed and excited that 300 children and their families participated. Each year, the celebration has grown with over 30,000 children attending the celebration in 2004. Martha Toscano, the Literacy Coordinator for the El Paso Public Library, says that the key ingredient of the celebration is books and kids. The celebration is organized and staffed by volunteers and staff from various agencies including the Parks and Recreation Department, the transit authority, the Police and Fire Departments, health agencies, the housing authority, children's organizations and local businesses.

The El Paso Public Library includes many interactive activities in their celebration—storytime, arts and crafts and fun learning games. Children have a card that gets stamped after they participate in an activity. If their card gets filled up, they receive a goodie bag. Each goodie bag has a free book, a fruit (fruit is a traditional item given in the Mexican celebration), some candy, information from participating agencies and a little toy. In addition to the activities, there is ongoing entertainment throughout the day showcasing talented kids in the community.

Organizing a large-scale Día de los Niños / Día de los Libros festival requires a collaboration of many agencies, volunteers and businesses. Ms. Toscano says that each year before the celebration many of her hard-working volunteers will tell her, "This is my last year. I can't do it any-more." But when they see how much fun the kids have and how impor-tant it is for them to receive a book, the volunteers get hooked again and sign up for the following year. Also, a network built around this type of celebration can be a year-long asset in promoting the library as a com-munity partner and resource.

RESOURCES

National Latino Children's Institute
Address: 1325 N. Flores Street, Suite 114, San Antonio, Texas 78212
Phone: 210-228-9997   *Fax:* 210-228-9972
Email: nlci@nlci.org
Website with information about Día de los Niños / Día de los Libros:
www.nlci.org/DLN2004/dlnintro2.htm

REFORMA
Website with information about Día de los Niños / Día de los Libros:
www.reforma.org/resources/ninos/dia.html

Texas Library Association
Address: 3355 Bee Cave Road, Suite 401, Austin, TX 78746-6763
Phone: 800-580-2852   *Fax:* 512-328-8852
Email: tla@txla.org
Website with info about Día de los Niños / Día de los Libros:
www.texasdia.org

RESOURCE ON SERVICES FOR LATINO YOUTH

Library Services to Youth of Hispanic Heritage, Edited by Barbara Immroth and Kathleen de la Peña McCook. McFarland and Company, Inc. (www.mcfarlandpub.com), 2000. ISBN 0-7864-0790-5
Description: This is a collection of essays about how best to meet the needs of young Latino library patrons.

LITERACY AND EDUCATION
If there are gaps in educational attainment or literacy in the Latino community that you serve, consider what resources or services the library can provide to help close the gap. Often there will be other community agencies working on these issues that you can partner with in order to provide quality services. Depending on where the gaps are in education or literacy, services that you might consider hosting or developing include tutoring or mentoring for children by community volunteers, family-centered literacy programs, General Educational Development (GED) classes in English or Spanish or English as a Second Language (ESL) classes.

Family Literacy Programs. The goal of family literacy programs is to sow a love of reading and a love of story within the family and community tradition. Children learn the value and joy of reading from their parents, and parents are encouraged to include reading in their family time.

In his description of a family literacy project started in Independence, Oregon, to work with immigrant families from México, Dick Keis suggests that the guiding principle for a successful family literacy program is that "the home language and culture of the families involved must be valued and respected as an integral part of the multicultural fabric of American society. Parents, as their children's first and foremost teachers, must be viewed as 'funds of knowledge' whose life experiences deserve to be shared with their children and need to be included as part of a meaningful curriculum." One effective way to do this is to include literature that is in the family's native language and that is culturally relevant to the parent and the child.[4]

The El Paso Public Library has launched a successful literacy program aimed at encouraging parents to read to their newborns called "*Estoy aprendiendo* / I am learning." Working in collaboration with area hospitals, parents of newborns are told that if they sign up their child for a library card at the nearest branch, they will receive a cute newborn t-shirt with the phrase "*Estoy aprendiendo*" on it. When parents come in to sign up their newborns for a library card and t-shirt, the librarians ask them if the parents and other children have library cards. They show the parents the board books and talk to them about the benefits of reading to their babies.

RESOURCES

Latino Family Literacy Project (LFLP)
Description: The Latino Family Literacy Project provides programs and training designed to establish family reading routines for Spanish- and English-speaking parents and their children. LFLP uses the VISTA Method, a language acquisition and a step-by-step literacy instruction process that involves family reading, vocabulary development and English-language development for Latino parents and their children. The Latino Family Literacy Project provides a trainer-of-trainers model for developmental programs designed to meet the specific literacy development of children ages birth to ten.
Address: 1107 Fair Oaks Ave. Suite 225, South Pasadena, CA 91030

Phone: 626-799-7341   *Fax:* 626-799-3851
Email: info@latinoliteracy.com
Website: www.latinoliteracy.com

Prime Time Family Reading Time®

Description: Prime Time is a family literacy program that was started by the Louisiana Endowment for the Humanities as a vehicle to bring people who were not currently using the libraries into the libraries. Based on its success in Louisiana, the program has grown and diversified with new curriculum and formats geared toward Latinos and Spanish-speakers.

Prime Time is a 6- or 8-week reading, discussion and storytelling program held at public libraries. A university scholar and a storyteller conduct weekly book discussion and storytelling sessions based on high-quality children's books. The program helps parents and children bond together around the act of reading. Parents and children read books together and discuss humanities topics (history, literature and ethical issues) related to the stories. The program also includes an introduction to libraries and library use.

The staff at Prime Time will work with libraries which are interested in the program to identify sources of funding for the program and will provide grant templates for use in seeking funding. Prime Time staff also provides training, curriculum, support and marketing materials to implement the program.

Contact: Faye Flanagan
Address: Louisiana Endowment for the Humanities
938 Lafayette Street, Suite 300, New Orleans, LA 70113
Phone: 504-523-4352   *Fax:* 504-529-2358
Email: flanagan@leh.org
Website: www.leh.org/primetime/PThomepage.htm

English as a Second Language (ESL). Many libraries partner with community colleges or universities to provide ESL classes at the library. Bruce Jensen, an ESL instructor, says "to draw linguistic minorities to your facility, you couldn't do much better than to offer ESL instruction."

One of the beauties of adult education is its patent lack of rigidity, the fact that it need not remotely resemble your grade school training. Even that label *adult education* sounds too restrictive—I've never taught a night class where kids weren't welcome. Some adult students don't have a choice about bringing children—either they can't get a babysitter, or they want that kid sitting right beside them for a sense of security. Your mileage may vary, so your policies will have to fit your library. It's a given, though, that the classroom should—like the rest of the building—be as comfortable and accommodating as you can manage. Plenty of chairs and hot coffee are a pretty good start. Similarly, your outreach purposes are best served by wide-open enrollment that expects learners to show up when they can and drop out when they must. This means more students going through the class, many of whom might just continue to patronize the library once they know where it is, and have felt its aspect change from mysterious and forbidding to warm and welcoming.

Cooperate with the teacher, and expect the same in return. Good educators are always hungry for inspiration—show off the resources you have for instructors and learners. Offer to help incorporate the library itself in lessons. Encourage the teacher to see to it—systematically, if necessary—that new students get library cards and know how to use them. Contemporary language teaching emphasizes experiential, communicative language use in practical contexts. The exercise of applying for a library card fits these criteria and is likely to be embraced by your instructor, who might even be inspired to build a lesson around the procedure.[5]

The Boulder Public Library developed a program called "Conversations in English" as a result of library users wanting to develop their conversational skills. The program is run by volunteers who are English speakers. Volunteers were trained about cultural mores and communication styles so that well-intentioned mistakes did not spoil interest in the program. The conversations were organized around "Easy Reading" titles (books written for adults learning English) and English as a Second Language library collections including books, magazines, newsletters, audio and video material.[6]

In a community with a growing population of Spanish speakers many English speakers will want to learn Spanish. Use Spanish speakers as a resource or as teachers and offer Spanish as a Second Language courses. Host conversations in Spanish and English to encourage limited-English speakers to speak to limited-Spanish speakers and vice versa. These conversations can be led by a bilingual facilitator who encourages everyone to communicate in their second language. Efforts like this help build community between Spanish speakers and English speakers who are often isolated from each other because of the language barrier.

Computer Resources and Classes. Computer resources and classes are popular with all library users. Make sure that these resources are easily accessible to Latino library users and to Spanish-language speakers. Add Spanish-language computer classes to your offerings. Make sure that your computer resource staff is familiar with Spanish search engines and Spanish Internet services such as www.espanol.yahoo.com and www.google.com/intl/es.

Larry Maynard, Spanish Outreach Coordinator for Glendale Public Library, said that staying in touch is important for the Latino library users that he serves. "Latinos love to chat online and email friends and family back home."

RESOURCES

WorldLinQ
Description: WorldLinQ is a multilingual web-based information system that provides information from countries throughout the world on the following topics: Arts and Humanities, Business and Economy, Education, Employment, Entertainment and Popular Culture, Government, Health and Medicine, History and Biography, Newspapers and Magazines, Science and Technology, Social Sciences and Sports and Leisure. Latinos especially enjoy the feature that connects them to newspapers from their country of origin.
Website: www.worldlinq.org

Latin American Network Information Center (LANIC)
Description: LANIC's mission is to facilitate access to Internet-based information to, from, or on Latin America.
Website: www.lanic.utexas.edu

ALSC: The Association for Library Service to Children
Description: ALSC's "Great Websites for Kids" features Spanish-language websites for children.
Website: www.ala.org/ala/alsc/greatwebsites/greatwebsiteslugares.htm

CULTURAL CELEBRATIONS, EVENTS AND COMMUNITY GATHERINGS
Use the library as a space for community gatherings and cultural celebrations and events. Tie these gatherings and celebrations to books and resources the library offers. These events will distinguish the library as an important community center for Latinos.

Holidays and Celebrations. Traditional Latino holidays and celebrations present an opportunity to highlight Latino culture and to tie the event to books and other library resources. For a non-traditional book display, ask someone in the community to build an alter for Día de los Muertos to remember important Latino and Latin American authors who have died such as Pablo Neruda, Sor Juana, Roque Dalton, Ricardo Sanchez, Arturo Islas, José Antonio Burciaga or others with whom the Latino community identifies.

Ghada Elturk, the outreach librarian for Boulder Public Library, cautions against "celebrating" ethnic cultures.

> One of the goals of our library's Outreach Program has been to avoid 'celebrating' a certain culture at a certain month or day and then forget about it for the rest of the year. It is our belief that cultural celebrations should be left to the people in the community to decide whether or not they want to share with the rest of us. Further, some 'celebrations' can be, and have been, offensive when performed by people outside the originating culture. Moreover, some aspects of a culture or ritual are properly performed in special settings. I believe the library's role is to have the right materials (for example, books, videos, tapes and posters) available and to make meeting rooms and other spaces available for people to use. All diverse cultural events and celebrations the library has offered through our Outreach Program have been initiated by people from the originating cultures and were not imposed from the library.[7]

RESOURCE

The Latino Holiday Book: From Cinco de Mayo to Día de los Muertos—
The Celebrations and Traditions of Latino-Americans, Second Edition.
By Valerie Menard. Marlow & Company (www.marlowepub.com), 2004,
ISBN 1-56924-406-5

Hispanic Heritage Month. Hispanic Heritage Month begins on September 15, the anniversary of independence for five Latin American countries— Costa Rica, El Salvador, Guatemala, Honduras and Nicaragua. México declared its independence on September 16, and Chile on September 18. Hispanic Heritage Month is a time dedicated to learning more about

Latino history and culture. Hispanic Heritage Month activities can include readings, panel discussions about important Latino issues, lectures by local Latino historians or professors, slide shows by Latino artists, Latin American movie showings and other events that highlight the history of Latin America and the history of Latinos in the United States. Use local university and community college professors as resources for developing these programs. Highlight books about Latino culture and history.

RESOURCES

Hispanic Heritage Awards
Description: The most prestigious celebration of Latino America's rich and vibrant contributions to our nation, the Hispanic Heritage Awards celebrates the achievements of outstanding Latino Americans in the arts, literature, leadership, education and sports, plus a lifetime achievement award.
> *Sponsor Organization:* Hispanic Heritage Awards Foundation
> *Address:* 2600 Virginia Ave NW, Suite #406, Washington, DC 20037
> *Phone:* 202-861-9797   *Fax:* 202-861-9799
> *Email:* contact@hispanicheritageawards.org
> *Website:* www.hispanicawards.org

Education World
Description: Education World has a lesson plan that is useful in developing children's programs and themes around Hispanic Heritage month.
> *Website:* www.education-world.com/a_lesson/lesson023.shtml

Cultural Events. Use Latino cultural events as a way to bring Latinos into your library. For example, in the Mexican American tradition, a girl's fifteenth birthday (quinceañera) is a very important and celebrated community and family event. If the quinceañera tradition is prevalent in your community, develop an event promoting Latina coming-of-age titles and books about quinceañeras—maybe a fashion show of quinceañera dresses; or a local historian or community leader talking about the various customs and traditions; or a display of photos from the community of quinceañeras from different generations.

When highlighting books for holidays or specific topics, make sure that Latino titles are represented. For example, if displaying books for Memorial Day or Veteran's day, include books that speak about the experience of

Latino veterans such as *Soldados, Chicanos in Viet Nam*, by Charley Trujillo and *A Patriot After All: The Story of a Chicano Viet Nam Vet*, by Juan Ramirez.

Ask Latinos in your community to use the library to share their culture with the rest of the community. Ghada Elturk, the Outreach Librarian for the Boulder Public Library, developed a program at the request of volunteers called the "Faces of Latin American Life." The series was suggested because volunteers from Latin American countries were

> constantly puzzled when people approach them with questions about a certain aspect of their lives, not realizing that the traditions, foods and celebrations of Venezuela, for one example, are often quite different from those of México or Puerto Rico . . .
>
> The series has been presented on a monthly basis, and has always promoted library materials and web sites related to the subjects being highlighted. Topics included national foods, heroes, holidays and independence days, social celebrations, music, dance and costumes, religious celebrations and discussions of santos, Milagros and Día de los Muertos. The volunteers have worked on the content and the style of the presentations. The librarian's role has been to book a library meeting room for the occasion, purchase materials as needed, advertise the event and be around if assistance is needed.[8]

Martha Toscano, the Literacy Coordinator for the El Paso Public Library, says some of her best cultural programming comes from her own curiosity about her family's heritage. Her parents grew up in México and would often talk about celebrating the Posada at Christmas, but they didn't celebrate it once they moved to the United States. A Posada is a celebration in which people go from door to door as Mary and Joseph did asking in song for a place to stay the night. At the last door, Mary and Joseph are welcomed in and the baby Jesus is to be celebrated. One year, Ms. Toscano asked people in the neighborhood to come to the library and celebrate the Posada there. A potluck feast, music and the traditional Posada make this one of the library's most well-attended community event.

People love to reconnect to their cultural heritage if those ties have been severed or the cultural tradition has been lost. The library can act as a resource for people wanting to reconnect to or know more about their cultural traditions.

Book Clubs and Author Readings. Book clubs are a great way to create a sense of community. Host book clubs in your library that are specific to Latinos. An example of a long-running, well-attended book club at a bookstore in El Paso is the Sor Juana Inés de la Cruz Book Club. Sor Juana was a Mexican poet and writer whose work is well known throughout Latin America and the United States. In celebration of Sor Juana, the book club reads original works in Spanish by Latin American women authors. The library can provide a comfortable place for book clubs to meet, help book club members select titles and publicize meeting times for the group.

RESOURCES

Human Pursuits
Description: Human Pursuits, a non-profit organization, provides bilingual discussion group materials free of charge.
    *Address:*1965 E. 3300 S., Salt Lake City, UT 84106
    Phone: 801-467-4220   *Fax:* 801-466-0834
    Email: humanpursuits@yahoo.com
    Website: www.humanpursuits.bluestep.net

Readings and booksignings by Latinos writers can be a big draw for a library if the events are well publicized. Let publishers know that you are interested in hosting readings and booksignings by Latino writers. To maximize resources and publicity efforts, host readings with community partners such as a university, community college or bookstore. If you are interested in hosting a writer from a particular Latin American country, contact the consulate from that country. Consulates often have resources available to promote their culture in the United States.

LIBRARY ASSISTANCE AND SERVICES FOR SPANISH SPEAKERS
If there are a lot of Spanish speakers in your service area, consider providing library services in Spanish. Provide a reference hotline for Spanish speakers, or, if that's not possible, make it a policy that if a Spanish speaker calls and doesn't immediately get assistance in Spanish that they get a phone call back by the end of the day. Provide a Spanish translation of

your website. Examples of library websites in Spanish can be found on the REFORMA website at www.reforma.org/spanishwebsites.htm.

Queens Library, one of New York City's three independent library systems, has developed a Mail-a-Book service for Spanish speakers who might feel apprehensive about accessing the library services because of the language barrier. Lists of Spanish-language titles are provided to anyone who would like to use the service. Books are selected from the list and are then mailed to the person's home free of charge with a pre-addressed stamped envelope to be used to return the book. Many of people who use this service end up coming to the library to find out more about the books and services available.

RESOURCES

Library Service to Spanish Speaking Patrons : A Practical Guide.
By Sharon Chickering Moller. Libraries Unlimited (www.lu.com), 2001.
ISBN 1563087197
Description: This is a resource for librarians who are planning and implementing services for Spanish speakers.

SERVICES THAT CONNECT LATINOS AND NEW IMMIGRANTS TO THE COMMUNITY

If Latinos in your service area are isolated or if there are a lot of new immigrants in your community, an important role for the library might be providing services that connect Latinos to the rest of the community.

Many libraries have taken an active role in helping new immigrants navigate and understand their new communities. Some of the most successful programs for new Americans are informational programs that help immigrants adapt to life in America. Depending on what immigrants are interested in learning about, topics can include immigration, health, employment, taxes, housing and tenants' rights.

Providing citizenship classes, information about voting in Spanish and information about community resources and organizations are other ways to connect Latinos and new immigrants to the community. Ask an immigration attorney to volunteer to provide citizenship classes or sessions on immigration law. Many libraries have developed online resources for new immigrants and Latinos. One example is Queens Library which developed a website called ¡Bienvenidos a Queens! (www.bienvenidosaqueens.org). The bilingual website features comprehensive information about community organizations, community resources and topics of interest to Latinos and new immigrants in the Queens Library service area. You can host community resource fairs and bring in representatives from agencies and organizations that new Americans want to know more about.

RESOURCES

U.S. Citizenship and Immigration Services
Description: This federal agency works to promote an understanding of the civic principles on which this nation was founded and increase public awareness of the benefits and responsibilities associated with U.S. Citizenship.

Website: www.uscis.gov
English Guide to Naturalization:
www.uscis.gov/graphics/services/natz/English.pdf
Spanish Guide to Naturalization:
www.uscis.gov/graphics/services/natz/Spanish.pdf

Chapter 4

Outreach and Publicity

Generate excitement and interest about your library, services, programs and activities in the Latino community.

YOU CAN build a really great Spanish-language collection. You can put together great programs that engage Latinos. You can provide useful services. You can have helpful and enthusiastic bilingual staff. But all of this great effort will only be as good as the time, thought and resources that you spend publicizing your library in the Latino community.

It is important to understand publicity as a continual process of letting people know what the library does. Publicity is the press release you send out to the media, the fliers you hand out in the community, the time you spend speaking to organizations and individuals about what the library offers, the quality of the services and programs that you offer and the friendly face that greets people when they enter the library. All of these things inform people about your library so all of these things need attention and thought.

Latinos in your community may have different media sources and word-of-mouth networks than you usually use to promote events. Take time to find out how people in the Latino community find out about events and what is going on in the community.

Publicity Through Informal Social Networks

Informal networks are often the most effective way to get out information about the library. People are more likely to respond to a recommendation from a friend or colleague than to an advertisement or a flier, especially if they are not yet familiar with the library. Identify informal social networks in the Latino community built around organizations or well-liked and well-respected individuals.

There are important connectors in any community who people depend on for information. Connectors are usually friendly people who everyone knows. As part of the way that they build relationships with others, connectors collect and share information. Find out who these people are in the Latino community and make sure to keep them informed about your library. Include these connectors on your library board or on an advisory council. Send them email or fax alerts about upcoming events. Add them to your mailing list. Talk to them often.

Yolanda Cardenas-Parra, the Library Circulation Section Supervisor at the City of Commerce Library in California, noticed that even though the Latino community was large and growing that very few Latinos were using the library. In response, she implemented a program called "*Embajadores /* Ambassadors" to help her promote the library in the Latino community. She asked the branch managers to identify two Latinos who were outgoing and who were regular library users. She met with these identified connectors and asked them to help her promote the library. She asked them for ideas on how best to do outreach in the community. She provided them with a comprehensive review of all the library had to offer. And then she asked them to share what they learned with people in their community.

The *embajadores'* job was to go back to their community and look for opportunities to educate people about the library and what it had to offer. For example, if an *embajador* was talking to a neighbor who was complaining that there were not enough things to do with her children, the *embajador* would mention all of the great library programs for children. Not only did this help in promoting the library, it helped to eliminate many of the barriers to use by letting people know that the libraries are for everybody and that everyone is welcome.

Because Cardenas-Parra designed the *embajadores* outreach project to be informal, fun and responsive to the *embajadores'* ideas and input, it has taken on a life of its own with the *embajadores* becoming involved in developing programming and helping to pass out library literature at community events. The *embajadores* set their own goals and their own agenda with support from Cardenas-Parra. She says that the *embajadores* program has been an invaluable tool that has increased Latino participation in the library—"The project has opened new doors and new ways of reaching out to the public."

Trusted businesses or community organizations also play a role in information sharing. Identify businesses or community organizations such as churches, non-profits, community centers, Hispanic Chambers of Commerce and schools that are an integral part of the Latino community. Ask these organizations or businesses to play a role in promoting the library. Ask them if they have a community calendar, a newsletter or a community board where information about the library can be posted. Ask them to co-host events. Make sure that these organizations or businesses receive fliers about events. Be creative about how to use these liaisons to get the word out about the library. For example, a popular fast-food chain in San Antonio agreed to use paper placemats that included information about the library on all of their food trays.

Teachers and school librarians are always willing to let students know about events and opportunities that they think will keep kids engaged in the learning process. Send teachers and school librarians fliers that they can copy and send home to parents. Get to know bilingual education teachers, dual language teachers and migrant education teachers. Put teachers and school librarians on your mailing lists. Ask them for input on programming and services. Ask them to bring their classes to the library. Ask them if you can come to their classrooms to talk about the library and sign children up for library cards.

Promote your library at local Latino festivals, gatherings and community centers. Linda Garcia, the Children's Librarian at Omaha Public Library in Nebraska, said that marketing to Latinos is "definitely a different marketing than we ever have done. We were caught up in programming as a way to bring people into the library. We are finding out that we need to go out into the community, where the people and the children are. I attend open houses at schools. I pass out fliers at organizations, churches, grocery stores and fiestas. I have found that Latinos need a personal contact. They need a face, someone who speaks Spanish. I get a much better response to the library after people have met me out in the community."

Larry Maynard, the Spanish Outreach Coordinator for the Glendale Public Library in Colorado, also commented, "The more you take yourself out of your comfort zone in the library and put yourself in their world, the more success you will have. I have a done a lot of programs offsite to establish relationships and trust. Then people are more comfortable coming to the library once they know a friendly face will be there who speaks Spanish."

MEDIA PUBLICITY
Media outlets that respond to the particular demands of the Latino population can be found in many communities throughout the United

States. Media formats might include bilingual or Spanish-language production of news and information, or news and information from the Latino perspective. Finding opportunities to highlight your programming and your library through these media outlets on a continuing basis will help you to build an identity in the Latino community.

In your community, it is important to become familiar with Spanish-language radio, television, Internet and print media and Latino-specific radio, television, Internet and print media. Spanish-language media is often more interested in news about cultural programs than English-language media.

Spend some time getting to know the editors and reporters for these media outlets. Invite them out to your library for an introduction. Let them know what you are trying to do. Ask them for their ideas. Ask them what kind of information and news they want to focus on. Ask them for the best way to get story ideas noticed. How soon in advance do they want to know about the event? Do they prefer email or faxed media releases? Do they prefer media releases in Spanish? Do they produce and broadcast public service announcements (PSAs)? What types of events will be a considered for a PSA?

Put these outlets on your media list, and keep them informed about upcoming events. If you think an event is especially important, ask broadcast media to produce and air a PSA. Always follow up a media release with a friendly phone call and an invitation to attend the event. When the media attends events, help them to find people to talk with about the library. In short, you will find great allies in the media when you actively help them put together a good story for their audience.

As a courtesy to Spanish-language media, Jack Galindo, the Public Relations Coordinator at the El Paso Public Library, provides Spanish-language media releases. This saves the media the time of translating material into Spanish for their audience. If you don't have the capacity to do this, most Spanish-language media have the capacity to translate material from English to Spanish.

Also, if the Latino population in your area is really growing, the traditional media will be looking for stories or ideas that will bring them a Latino audience. Look for ideas about Latino authors, Latino-focused reading groups or other events to pitch to this media.

LIBRARY SIGNAGE

Library signage is a subtle, important and necessary way to communicate that the library welcomes Spanish speakers. If you have bilingual staff, put a big sign outside saying "*Bienvenidos. Se habla español*" and include this phrase in promotional material. This is a great way of letting Latinos, specifically Spanish speakers, know that they are welcome and will feel comfortable in your library.

To help Spanish speakers navigate the library, make sure that all directional and informational signs are in Spanish as well as English. It is also important that the placement and the size of the signs are given equal weight and value as the signs in English. If you don't pay attention to this, you may inadvertently send the wrong message. For example, I was in a public building once where two signs in Spanish and English asked people to put their trash in a garbage can. Because the Spanish sign was much larger and was in a much bolder font, the message I took from that was that the officials who put it there thought that Spanish speakers were more likely to litter.

Translate library forms, documents, informational brochures and your website into Spanish. Include the phrase "gratis/free" on promotional material if you know that many Latinos in your community don't know that library services are free.

RESOURCES

PLUS, Public Libraries Using Spanish
Description: On their website, PLUS (Public Libraries Using Spanish) has library forms, documents and signage in Spanish.
Website: www.sol-plus.net/plus/home.htm

DEVELOPING PROMOTIONAL MATERIAL

If a large portion of your target market speaks Spanish, develop bilingual promotional material. The best approach to developing bilingual material is to include Spanish on one side of a flier and English on the other side. This gives the Spanish and English equal weight and importance.

It also makes the text easier to read. Bilingual formats where the languages are in different fonts or where one language is in italics and the other is not can be confusing and hard to read. It is very important when translating English into Spanish for publicity purposes that the translation is accurate and authentic. A poor translation can seriously undermine your efforts. Make sure that the Spanish is reflective of the Spanish spoken in the local community and reflective of your audience's preference for formal or informal Spanish. It is important to be aware of regional variances in Spanish. Make sure that the material is well-edited with proper punctuation and accents in place. Never use computer software to translate material.

Promotional material should be culturally sensitive. Don't use offensive or stereotypical imagery or symbols. Ask community volunteers to help you create high quality promotional material that will be well received in the Latino community.

RESOURCES

OLOS: The Office for Literacy and Outreach Services
Description: OLOS serves the American Library Association by supporting and promoting literacy and equity of information access initiatives for traditionally underserved populations. This website has useful information and ideas to help you strengthen your outreach initiatives.
Website: www.ala.org/ala/olos/literacyoutreach.htm

Chapter 5

ACCESS

*Provide comfortable and easy access to the library for
the local Latino community.*

ONCE you have grabbed the attention and interest of Latinos, it is important to make sure that the library is user-friendly and comfortable for Latinos. Your library should be welcoming to Latinos. Make sure that cultural and language barriers don't stand in the way of a library user accessing the services they need. It is important that Latinos feel ownership of the library. Every aspect of the library should say loudly and clearly, "The library belongs to everyone. *La biblioteca es para todos.*"

Make an honest assessment of what real and perceived barriers to use of the library might be. Libraries are critical institutions in building strong communities. Because of this, it is important that libraries play a lead role in bringing together all different segments of the community and making sure that everyone knows they are welcome to use the library. As communities change, libraries respond to that change. They change to reflect the needs and characteristics of the community. This change can often create confusion and tension. It is important to remember that good will, a fearless heart and a willingness to listen are critical to building a patron base that feels welcome in your library and in your community.

Educate your staff about your efforts to increase Latino participation of the library. Discourage staff from making broad generalizations about Latinos. Encourage them to see each individual as unique and as a potential loyal patron who is entitled to courtesy and respect. Often when working within a community that you are just getting to know, there will be misunderstandings that can potentially lead to hard feelings. Be direct and deal with conflict or library users' concerns quickly, encouraging frank and honest discussion about the problem.

IMMIGRANTS

Many new immigrants may think that their citizenship status prevents them from accessing the library. There is no federal law that precludes an "undocumented resident" or someone who has not established full citizenship from using the library. If your policy for granting library cards doesn't allow residents who have not yet established full citizenship to use the library, consider making changes that eliminate barriers to use. For example, some libraries in communities with many Mexican residents accept the Matricula Consular (Mexican Consulate I.D.) in tandem with other documents that demonstrate residency (property tax bill, school ID, bills, etc.) The Matricula Consular card is a photo identification issued by the Mexican Consulate for Mexican Nationals living in the United States.

Interacting with public institutions can be colored with fear and confusion for new immigrants. These feelings may prevent many new immigrants from using the library. An understanding of this confusion and fear and a willingness to go out into the community will help ease some of these concerns.

THE FACE AND THE LANGUAGE OF THE LIBRARY

The atmosphere and the nature of a place is always defined by people. Who works and who doesn't work at your library sends a message about what kind of a place your library is. Even though it might not be intended, it also sends a message about who is welcome at your library. Because of this, recruiting and hiring Latino librarians and Spanish-speaking librarians is critical to providing welcoming access for Latinos. This is especially true if Latinos are isolated culturally and geographically from other sectors of the community. Seeing one's culture included in collections, programming and staffing helps build a sense of ownership and belonging.

If your service area includes a sizable population of Spanish speakers, your number one resource priority should be hiring Spanish-speaking library staff. Accessing the library will always be a problem for Spanish speakers if you do not have knowledgeable Spanish speakers on your staff. As a stop-gap measure, you can teach English-only speakers on your staff rudimentary library Spanish or recruit Spanish-speaking volunteers, but this will never prove adequate to the task of providing full, comfortable and welcoming access to the library.

Bruce Jensen of PLUS recounted visiting a branch library in a lively Latino neighborhood in California. He said the branch library was like a "well-lighted tomb." He couldn't figure out why—the library had Spanish signage and a first-rate collection of books and videos in Spanish. "We discovered the missing piece after about 20 minutes, when I heard the reference librarian say loudly across the desk, 'I DON'T SPEAK SPANISH,' to some guy who just wanted something simple." If the library is committed to serving Spanish speakers, it must hire Spanish-speaking librarians and staff.

Even though Latinos represent 13% of the population, only 3.5% of librarians are Latinos, and Latinos are also underrepresented in library degree programs.[1] Because of this, your job in recruiting Latinos and Spanish speakers to work at your library will also include recruiting Latinos and Spanish speakers to the library profession. Identify and mentor Latino talent in your community. Counsel Latinos interested in the library profession about available scholarships, educational opportunities and career paths. Make sure that the library profession is represented at job fairs and career days.

RESOURCES

REFORMA
Description: REFORMA has a frequently updated employment database where libraries can post job opportunities.
    Website: www.reforma.org/refoempl.htm
REFORMA also has a scholarship program.
    Website: www.reforma.org/scholarship.htm

Spectrum Initiative of the American Library Association
Description: Spectrum is an initiative "designed to address the specific issue of underrepresentation of critically needed ethnic librarians within the profession." Spectrum's most important effort is recruiting and providing scholarships to promising students. The Spectrum website also includes tips and resources on recruiting for diversity.
    Website: www.ala.org/spectrum

Spanish-Language Marketplace

This directory of the Spanish-language marketplace was compiled by *Críticas, An English Speaker's Guide to the Latest Spanish Language Titles. Críticas* is a comprehensive review of the latest in Spanish-language publishing written in English. More information about the industry is available at www.criticasmagazine.com

Wholesaler and Distributors

ABC's Book Supply, Inc.
7301 West Flagler St.
Miami, FL 33144-2505
Phone: 305-262-4240
Fax: 305-262-4115
Website: www.abcsbook.com
Email: abcsbook@abcsbook.com
Special Products: Classroom Décor,
K-University Textbooks, Literature Books,
Supplemental Materials
Special Services: Cataloging

Acme Agency, S.A.
Suipacha 245
Buenos Aires, C1008AAE, Argentina
Phone: 54-11-4328-1662
Fax: 54-11-4328-9345
Email:
acme@redynet.com.ar
Special Products: Children's and Young
Adult Books
Catalog Description: Children's, Young
Adult and Adult Books, CDs, DVDs, Videos
and Magazines.
Titles Stocked: 300

Advanced Marketing, S. A. de R.L. de C.V.
Aztecas #33, Col. Sta. Cruz Acatlán
Naucalpan, 53150, México
Phone: 52-55-5360-3139
Fax: 52-55-5360-5851
Website: www. advmkt.com
Email: carlosl@advmkt. com

Special Products: Art, Children's Books,
Cookbooks
Catalog Description: Catalog available with
annotations in English.
Titles Stocked: 150
Special Services: Worldwide distribution of
books in Spanish

AIMS International Books, Inc.
7709 Hamilton Av.
Cincinnati, OH 45231
Phone: 1-800-733-2067
Fax: 513-521-5592
Website: www.aimsbooks.com
Email: aimsbooks@fuse.net
Special Products: Spanish
Titles Stocked: 1,000

Aliform Publishing
117 Warwick St. SE
Minneapolis, MN 55414
Phone: 612-379-7639
Fax: 612-379-7639
Website: www. aliformgroup.com
Email: information@aliformgroup.com
Special Products: Latin American and
Mexican Literature
Has Publisher Exclusivity: Praxis (México)
Titles Stocked: 40

American Wholesale Book Company
131 25th St. South
Irondale, AL 35210
Phone: 205-956-4151

Fax: 205-956-5530
Email: SastoqueL@awbcinc.com
Special Products: All Subjects
Titles Stocked: 1,500

Astran, Inc.
P. O. Box 490274
Key Biscayne, FL 33149
Phone: 305-597-0064
Fax: 305-597-0047
Website: www. astranbooks.com
Email: sales@astranbooks.com
Special Products: Books in Spanish
Titles Stocked: 3,500

Asunto Impreso
Pasaje Rivarola, 169
Buenos Aires, Argentina
Phone: 54-11-4-383-6262
Fax: 54-11-4-383-5152
Website: www.asuntoimpreso.com
Email: www@asuntoimpreso.com
Special Products: Architecture, Art, Design
and Fashion, Photography

Audio Video Latino
2213 Sunset Crest Dr.
Los Angeles, CA 90046
Phone: 323-656-4665
Fax: 323-656-4665
Website: www.AudioVideoLatino.com
Email: sales@AudioVideoLatino.com
Special Products: Children's Educational
CDs, DVDs, Games, Software, Videos
Catalog Description: Educational Books,
Tapes, Disks and Software in Spanish for the
young and the young at heart
Titles Stocked: 400

Baker & Taylor
2709 Water Ridge Parkway
Charlotte, NC 28217
Phone: 800-775-1800
Website: www.btol.com
Email: btinfo@btol.com
Special Products: Music, Print, Spoken
Word, Video
Catalog Description: Catalog available for
Spanish books, music, and Video/DVD.

Catalog descriptions are written in English.
Database available online with a subscription.
Titles Stocked: 11,000
Special Services: Cataloguing and Processing,
Collection Development lists, The Title
Source II™, Value Added Services

Bilingual Books for Kids, Inc.
PO Box 653 Ardsley, NY 10502
Phone: 914-524-7325
Fax: 914-524-7325 Website:
www.bilingualbooks.com Email:
bilingualbooks@mindspring.com
Special Products: Educational Materials,
Games, Language Learning Tapes for
Children, Young Adults, Students, and
Teachers, Music, Spanish and English/
Bilingual Books
Titles Stocked: 300

Bilingual Publications Co.
270 Lafayette St.
New York, NY 10012
Phone: 212-431-3500
Fax: 212-431-3567
Email: lindagoodman@juno.com
Special Products: Audio Books, Bilingual and
Spanish-language Children's Books, Original
Adult Fiction by Contemporary Latin
American Writers, Young Adult Fiction and
Nonfiction
Has Publisher Exclusivity:
Plaza y Valdés
Catalog Description: Contemporary Latin
American Fiction, U.S. Latino Fiction,
Fiction in Translation, Health, Parenting and
Computer Books
Titles Stocked: 80,000
Special Services: Annotated EXCEL lists,
Approval plans, Displays, Workshops

Bolivia Books
141 East 89th St., 3 L
New York, NY 10128
Phone: 212-289-9135
Fax: 212-289-9135
Email: boliviabooks@aol.com
Special Products:
Books from Bolivia

Catalog Description: Literature, History, Political and Social Studies, Indigenous Cultures, Art, Periodicals, Journals, and General Interest

Bookazine Co., Inc.
75 Hook Rd.
Bayonne, NJ 07002
Phone: 800-221-8112
Fax: 201-339-7778
Website: www.Bookazine.com
Email: info@Bookazine.com
Special Products: Business Books, Children's Books, Computer Books, Foreign-Language Titles, Gay and Lesbian Lifestyle Books, Regional Titles, Spanish Titles, Travel Titles
Catalog Description: General Interest Spanish-language titles for all Retail Environments. Combining titles from the most important Spanish-language publishers and distributors.
Titles Stocked: 5,000

Books, Information & Services, Inc. (BIS)
PO Box 60326
Houston, TX 77205
Phone: 52-55-5535-4041
Fax: 52-55-5535-7712
Email: rgreenwald@bislibros.com
Special Products: Children's Books, Fiction, Self-help, University Textbooks

Brodart Books & Automation
500 Arch St.
Williamsport, PA 17701
Phone: 800-233-8467
Fax: 570-326-1479
Website: www.brodart.com
Email: dmendonca@brodart.com
Catalog Description: Annotations in English of every title, with front cover photograph
Titles Stocked: 3,000
Special Services:
Shelf-ready custom cataloguing and processing

BWI
1847 Mercer Rd.
Lexington, KY 40511
Phone: 800-888-4478
Fax: 800-888-6319
Website: www.bwibooks.com
John Nelson, President
Special Products: Spanish and Spanish/English bilingual books (including graphic novels), books on tape, spoken word, music, VHS, and DVDs for children, young adults, and adults
Catalog Description: Spanish and Spanish/English products featured in our various catalogs
Titles Stocked: 3,331 Spanish book and AV titles and 670 bilingual Spanish/English book and AV titles on TitleTales (our online searchable database)
Special Services: free collection development services such as special lists prepared by MLS-degreed librarians; Selection, Notification, and Acquisition Plan (SNAP); Awards and Best Books Plan; Children's and YA Book Series Plan; Billboard Standing Order Plan; Children's Video Series Standing Order Plan; StreetWise Alert; BroadcastPremiere alert, a semi-monthly eNewsletter; book and AV reviews by our MLS-degreed staff and nine well-known industry journals; customized cataloging and processing; TitleTales (our online searchable database); downloadable free brief MARC bibs from TitleTales; full MARC Records; OCLC Cataloging Partner; Shelf-ready physical processing; BeeWee Bound editions; eBooks

Celesa
Laurel 21
Madrid, 28005, Spain
Phone: 34-91-517-0170
Fax: 34-91-517-3481
Website: www.celesa.com
Email: celesa@celesa.com
Catalog Description: Any book in Spanish from any publisher
Special Services: Thematic catalogs

Chulainn Publishing Corp.
7436 Indian Well Way
Lone Tree, CO 80124-4211
Phone: 303-790-7837
Fax: 303-790-7837

Email: chulainn.libros@att.net
Special Products: Books, AudioBooks and
Videos, Spanish Publications
Titles Stocked: 1,000

Consortium Book Sales & Distribution
1045 Westgate Dr., Suite 90
Saint Paul, MN 55114
Phone: 651-221-9035
Fax: 651-221-0124
Website:
www.cbsd.com
Special Products: Adult and Children's
Books, Audiobooks.
Catalog Description: Frontlist Catalogs
Include Annotations in English
Titles Stocked: 155

CWD México, S.A. de C.V.
Juan Kepler 4047, Col. Arboledas
Zapopán, 45070, México
Phone: 52-33-3809-5754
Fax: 52-55-5554-3215
Website: www.cwdmexico.com
Email: aramirez@cwdmexico.com
Special Products: Educational CD ROMs
Has Publisher Exclusivity:
Lectus Vergara, Edicinco, Emme, Acta, CN,
Aspel, Cristal
Catalog Description: Educational and
Cultural CD-ROMs for Children, Young
Adults, and Adults
Titles Stocked: 172

Distribuciones Plaza Mayor
1500 Ponce de Leon Ave., Local 2
El Cinco, San Juan, 00926, Puerto Rico
Phone: 787-764-0455
Fax: 787-764-0465
Website: www.editorialplazamayor.com
Email:
distribuciones@editorialplazamayor.com
Special Products: Dictionaries and
Encyclopedias, General Interest, Textbooks
Has Publisher Exclusivity: Grupo Anaya,
Grao, Diada, Diccionario de la Real
Academia Española, Urano, Emecé, Lafer
Catalog Description: Spanish Literature
Titles Stocked: 4,500

Distribuidora de Publicaciones Oveja Negra, Ltda.
Transversal 93, #62-46 Interior 16
Bogotá, Colombia
Phone: 571-252-9694
Fax: 571-434-4139
Website: www.distovejanegra.com
Email: dipon@andinet.com
Special Products: Children's and Young
Adult, Contemporary Literature, General
Interest, Politics and Economics
Has Publisher Exclusivity: Editorial Oveja
Negra LTDA
Catalog Description: Thematic collections
Titles Stocked: 1,600

Donars Spanish Books
PO Box 32205
Aurora, CO 80041
Phone: 800-552-3316
Fax: 303-343-7111
Email: donars@prolynx.com
Titles Stocked: 4,000
Special Services: Title Searches, Special
Orders

Downtown Book Center
247 SE 1st St.
Miami, FL 33131
Phone: 305-377-9941
Fax: 305-371-5926
Website: yp.bellsouth.com/sites/
downtownbooks/
Email: raxdown@aol.com
Special Products:
Adult Spanish Titles
Has Publisher Exclusivity: Dax Books
Catalog Description: Titles in Spanish of
General Interest and All Subjects
Titles Stocked: 10,000
Special Services: Brief and Full MARC
Records, Cataloguing with OCLC and
Physical Processing

DV & A
133 Candy Lane
Palm Harbor, FL 34683
Phone: 727-447-4147
Fax: 727-441-3069
Website: www.dva.com

Email: movies@dva.com
Special Products: Video and DVD
Catalog Description: Online monthly newsletter
Titles Stocked: 500
Special Services: Full Processing

Ediciones Colihue, S.R.L.
Ac. Diaz Velez 5125
Buenos Aires, C1405DCG, Argentina
Phone: 54-11-4-958-4442
Fax: 54-11-4-958- 5673
Website: www.colihue.com.ar
Email: ecolihue@colihue.com.ar
Special Products: Books from Latin America and Spain

Ediciones Norte, Inc.
PO Box 29461
San Juan, 00929-0461, Puerto Rico
Phone: 787-701-0909
Fax: 787-701-0922
Website: www.edicionesnorte.com
Email: info@edicionesnorte.com
Special Products:
Children's Books, Literature, Nutrition, Reference, Religion, Self-help, Textbooks
Has Publisher Exclusivity: Art Enterprise, DCOM
Titles Stocked: 131

Ediciones Universal
3090 SW 8th St.
Miami, FL 33135
Phone: 305-642-3355
Fax: 305-642-7978
Website: www.ediciones.com
Email: ediciones@ediciones.com
Special Products: Cuban Books
Catalog Description: Books from Latin America and Spain, Dictionaries and Reference
Titles Stocked: 100,000
Special Services: MARC Records, OCLC, Standing Orders

Edilar, S.A. de C.V.
Blvd. Manuel Avila Camacho 1994, Despacho 403
México City, México

Phone: 52-55-5361-9611
Fax: 52-55-5361-0851
Website: www.clublectores.com
Email: club@clublectores.com
Has Publisher Exclusivity: Programa Nacional de Bibliotecas Magisteriales (PNBM)
Titles Stocked: 300

Editorial Limusa, S.A. de C.V.
Balderas 95
México City, 06040, México
Phone: 52-8503-8050
Fax: 52-5512-2903
Website: www.noriega.com.mx
Email: limusa@noriega.com.mx
Special Products: Adult, Children's, and Young Adult Books
Has Publisher Exclusivity: Vicens Vives, Pila Telena
Catalog Description: Synopsis and technical information available
Titles Stocked: 200

Educational Record Center, Inc
3233 Burnt Mill Dr.
Wilmington, NC 28403
Phone: 800-438-4637
Fax: 888-438-1637
Website: www.erckids.com
Email: scott@erckids.com
Special Products: Audiobooks and Music, Children's Books, Videos in Spanish and English

F&G Editores/F&G Libros de Guatemala
31 Ave. C 5-54, Zona 7
Col. Centroamérica
Guatemala City, Guatemala
Phone: 502-433-2361
Fax: 502-433-2361
Website: www.fygeditores.com
Email: fgeditor@guate.net.gt
Special Products: Books from Guatemala.
Catalog Description: All of the books published in Guatemala since 2000
Titles Stocked: 300

Films for the Humanities & Sciences
PO Box 2053
Princeton, NJ 08534-2053

Phone: 800-257-5126
Fax: 609-671-5777
Website: www.films.com
Email: custserv@films.com
Special Products: CD-ROM, Culture, DVD, Literature, VHS
Has Publisher Exclusivity: BBC, Discovery, ABC News, and Public Affairs Television
Titles Stocked: 347
Special Services: All proprietary titles closed-captioned. Closed-circuit transmission rights granted upon request. Customer satisfaction guaranteed or return purchase within 30 days for full credit or refund. Digital licensing available for selected programs. Discounts offered for multiple copies or large volume orders.

Girón Books, Inc.
2130 W. 21st St.
Chicago, IL 60608
Phone: 773-847-3000
Fax: 773-847-9197
Website: www. gironbooks.com
Email: sales@gironbooks.com
Special Products: Biographies, Children, Cooking, Education, Family, Fiction, History, Humor, Music, Natural Healing, New Age, Parenting, Philosophy, Poetry, Psychology, Reference, Religion, Self-help, Sexual Education, Sports
Has Publisher Exclusivity: Girón Publishing, Ediciones Selectas Diamante, Selector, and Edamex
Catalog Description: Best-selling Spanish-language Books
Titles Stocked: 1,400
Special Services: The most effective distribution system for books in Spanish

Globus Publishing, LLC
5424 NW 94th, Doral Place
Miami, FL 33178
Phone: 305-718-8340
Fax: 305-718-8342
Email: nestorz@att.net
Special Products: Fiction, General Interest, Literature
Titles Stocked: 25

Gryphon House, Inc.
1076 Tucker St.
Beltsville, MD 20704
Phone: 301-595-9500
Fax: 301-595-0051
Website: www.ghbooks.com
Email: info@ghbooks.com
Special Products: Books for Teachers and Parents. Many of the titles are bilingual (English/Spanish) or in Spanish
Has Publisher Exclusivity: Teaching Strategies, Redleaf Press, Bright Ring Publishing
Catalog Description: Books for Early Childhood for Teachers and Parents
Titles Stocked: 26

Howard Karno Books, Inc.
PO Box 2100
Valley Center, CA 92082
Phone: 760-749-2304
Fax: 760-749-4390
Website: www.karnobooks.com
Email: info@karnobooks.com
Special Products: All Subjects pertaining to Latin America and the Caribbean, Archaeology, Architecture, Cinema, Cookbooks, Decorative Arts, Folk Art, Latin American Art, Music, Out-of-print and Antiquarian Materials, Photography
Catalog Description: Specialists in Materials from Latin America and the Caribbean
Titles Stocked: 14,000
Special Services: Approval and Blanket Order Plans, Collection Development.

Iberbook
Arquitecto Gaudi 1
Madrid, 28016, Spain
Phone: 34-91-359-2386
Fax: 34-91-350-8260
Website: www.iberbook.com
Email: customerserv@iberbook.com
Special Products: All Book Publications from Portugal. All library Materials/Media Published or Distributed in Spain
Catalog Description: Quarterly catalogs in various subject areas available online
Special Services: Airfreight/UPS Shipping to North America in 10-14 days, Free MARC

Bibs with Invoicing Data, New Title Announcements Via E-mail, Order Status Information Via Website, Special Website Database for Academic and Research Libraries, Special Website Database for Public Library Materials, Standing Orders

Ideal Foreign Books
132-10 Hillside Ave.
Richmond Hill, NY 11418
Phone: 718-297-7477
Fax: 718-297-7645
Website: idealforeignbooks@att.net
Special Products: Academic Materials, Spanish and Latin American literature
Titles Stocked: 2,000

iLeón.com (A Division of Verticalibros, LLC)
935 Genter St., #203
La Jolla, CA 92037
Phone: 858-688-6106
Fax: 858-456-0810
Website: www.ileon.com
Email: info@verticalibros.com, info@ileon.com
Titles Stocked: 55,000.
Special Services: Centralized solutions for international book acquisition. Access to an international network of more than 3,000 publishing houses. Start-up and custom collection development. Cataloging, MARC records, physical processing, and library binding services.

Ingram Book Group
One Ingram Blvd.
La Vergne, TN 37086
Phone: 800-937-8000
Fax: 615-213-4552
Website: www.ingrambook.com
Special Products: Audiobooks, Calendars, Hard-to-find Titles, Medical Reference, Music, Periodicals, Spanish-language Videos & DVDs
Titles Stocked: 25,000.
Special Services: Direct to Home delivery services for libraries at any valid U.S. address. Ingram's state-of-the-art bibliographic data is accessible through ipage™, the leading e-business website for the book industry.

Independent Publishers Group
814 N. Franklin St.
Chicago, IL 60610
Phone: 312-337-0747
Fax: 312-337-1807
Website: www.ipgbook.com
Email: frontdesk@ipgbook.com
Special Products: Adult and Children's Trade Titles
Has Publisher Exclusivity: Alfaomega Grupo Editor, Blume, Callis Editora, Combel Editorial, CSA Press, Ediciones Barataria
Catalog Description: 2 catalogs per year, also available online. Each frontlist title features color cover and copy in Spanish and English.
Titles Stocked: 750
Special Services: Library and Bookstore Signage Provided, Spanish Books can be Combined with English for Best Discount

Latin American Periodicals
2555 North Coyote Dr., Suite 109
Tucson, AZ 85745
Phone: 520-770-1130
Fax: 520-690-6574
Email: lapmagazines@worldnet.att.net
Special Products: Periodicals, Spanish-language Magazines
Has Publisher Exclusivity: Fotonovelas
Catalog Description: Hardcopy updated annually, with detailed description of each title, as for content, periodicity, and annual subscription price
Titles Stocked: 70
Special Services: Customized fotonovela and periodical packages geared towards specific demographic needs of libraries

LD Books, Inc.
8313 NW 68 ST
Miami, FL 33166
Phone: 305-406-2292
Fax: 305-406-2293
Email: ldbooks@bellsouth.net
Special Products:
Literature, Narrative, New Age

Has Publisher Exclusivity: Lectorum S.A. de CV, and Quarzo
Titles Stocked: 1,300

Lectorum Publications, Inc.
205 Chubb Ave.
Lyndhurst, NJ 07071
Phone: 800-345-5946
Fax: 877-532-8676
Website: www.lectorum.com
Special Products: Adult Fiction and Nonfiction, Children's Fiction and Nonfiction
Has Publisher Exclusivity: Edebe, Edelvives, Editorial Everest, Kokinos, Litexsa, Noguer, Salamandra, and Serres
Catalog Description: Children's Books in Spanish and English, Dictionaries and Encyclopedias, Adult Trade Catalog
Titles Stocked: 15,000
Special Services: Collection Development

Libromundo Spanish Book Distributor
5609 Beck Ave.
North Hollywood, CA 91601
Phone: 818-769-8252
Fax: 818-769-8252
Email: libromundo@msn.com
Special Products:
Bilingual Dictionaries, General Interest, Self-help
Titles Stocked: 1,800

Libros Sin Fronteras
PO Box 2085
Olympia, WA
Phone: 360-357-4332
Fax: 360-357-4964
Website: www.librossinfronteras.com
Email: info@librossinfronteras.com
Special Products: Audio and Video, Books of All Subjects and Age Groups
Catalog Description: Annotated catalog
Titles Stocked: 30,000
Special Services: MARC records, OCLC Cataloguing Partner, Shelf-ready Physical Processing

Liturgical Press
St John's Abbey
Collegeville, MN 656321

Phone: 800-858-5450
Fax: 800-445-5899
Website: www.litpress.org
Email: sales@litpress.org
Special Products: Catholic Books, Ecumenical Books
Has Publisher Exclusivity: Obra Nacional de la Buena Prensa
Catalog Description: Spanish-language Titles from Latin American Catholic and Ecumenical Publishers
Titles Stocked: 180

Mariuccia Iaconi Book Imports, Inc.
970 Tennessee St.
San Francisco, CA 94107
Phone: 800-955-9577
Fax: 415-821-1596
Website: www.iaconibooks.com
Email: mibibook@earthlink.net
Special Products: Children's Books
Has Publisher Exclusivity: Ediciones Tecolote
Catalog Description: Spanish-language Books for Newborns to Young Adults, Reference, Bilingual Books in Many Different Languages
Titles Stocked: 15,000
Special Services: Cataloging with OCLC

México Norte
4823 Meadow Dr., Suite 103
Durham, NC 27713
Phone: 919-361-0997
Fax: 919-361-2597
Website: www.vientos.com
Email: mexiconorte@vnet.net
Special Products: Mexican Books
Catalog Description: Titles organized by Mexican state. Books are listed with bibliographic information in Spanish
Titles Stocked: 7,500
Special Services: Approval Orders, Blanket Orders, U.S. MARC Records

Multi-Cultural Books & Videos
28880 Southfield Rd., Suite 183
Lathrup Village, MI 48076
Phone: 800-567-2220
Fax: 248-559-2465

Website: www.multiculturalbooksandvideos.com
Email: service@multiculbv.com
Special Products:
Adult and Children's Books, Children's
Bilingual Books, DVDs, Videos, and
Audiobooks
Catalog Description: Adult and Children's
Fiction and Nonfiction, Popular Films
Available on DVD
Titles Stocked: 1,500
Special Services: MARC Records, OCLC.
Partner's Program, Shelf-ready Processing

Noda Audio Visual
PO Box 24
Loveland, CO 80539
Phone: 970-532-3600
Fax: 970-532-7352
Email: nodav@msn.com
Special Products: Videos in Spanish
Has Publisher Exclusivity: Krismar
Computación
Titles Stocked: 600
Special Services: Data on request.

Pathfinder Press
PO Box 162767
Atlanta, GA 162767
Phone: 404-669-0600
Fax: 707-669-1411
Website: www.pathfinderpress.com
Email: orders@pathfinderpress.com
Special Products: Selected titles from Cuba,
Vladimir Lenin in Spanish, Writings of Karl
Marx
Titles Stocked: 150

Publications Exchange, Inc.
13351 SW 102 St.
Miami, FL 33186
Phone: 305-287-4957
Fax: 305-387-1954
Website: www.pexstore.com
Email: Pexusa@bellsouth.net
Special Products: Cuban Books.
Catalog Description: All Cuban Publishers
Titles Stocked: 1,300

Public Square Books
307 Seventh Ave., Suite 1601
New York, NY
Phone: 212-604-0446
Fax: 212-604-0390
Website: www.publicsquarebooks.com
Email: Katelin@publicsquarebooks.com
Special Products: Spanish-language Graphic
Novels
Has Publisher Exclusivity: Norma Editorial
of Spain
Catalog Description: Graphic Novels for
Children, Young Adults, and Mature
Audiences
Titles Stocked: 75

Publishers Group West
1700 Fourth St.
Berkeley, CA 94710
Phone: 510-528-1444
Fax: 510-528-3444
Website: www.pgw.com
Email: sandras@pgw.com
Special Products: Art and Architecture,
Décor, Health, Juvenile, Lifestyle and
Cooking, Personal Growth, Women's Issues
Has Publisher Exclusivity: The largest
exclusive distributor of independent
publishers in North America
Titles Stocked: 250

Santa Fe Books Corp.
2100 W. 76th St., Suite 401
Hialeah, FL 33016
Phone: 786-208-9787
Fax: 305-692-1797
Website: www.santafebooks.com
Email: info@santafebooks.com
Special Products: Books from Spain and
Latin America
Titles Stocked: 30,000
Special Services: 72-hour shipping

SBD Spanish Book Distributor, Inc.
6706 Sawmill Rd.
Dallas, TX 75252-5816
Phone: 800-609-2114
Fax: 888-254-6709
Website: www.sbdbooks.com
Email: sbd@sbdbooks.com

Special Products: Audio, Biography, Books for Adults, Young Adults, and Families, Business, CD-ROMs, Classics, Computer, Cooking, Dictionaries and Encyclopedias, Fiction, Health, Hispanic Authors, History, How-to, Parenting, Poetry, Religion, Romance, Self-help
Catalog Description: Bimonthly catalog (Spanish Book News) with over 300 of the newest titles
Titles Stocked: 10,000
Special Services: Grants for Libraries and Schools, Newsletters, Online Catalog, Online Clearance Sale, Standing Order, Top 10 of the Month, Worldwide Book Search

Siglo del Hombre Editores, S.A.
Cra. 32 #25-46
Bogotá, Colombia
Phone: 571-337-7700
Fax: 571-337-7665
Website: www.siglodelhombre.com
Email: gerencia@siglodelhombre.com
Special Products: Colombia's University Presses
Catalog Description: Books Published by University Presses and Various Organizations in Colombia
Titles Stocked: 655

Spanish Language Book Services Inc.
7855 NW 12th St., Suite 211
Miami, FL 33126
Phone: 305-437-9929
Fax: 305-437-9881
Website: www.slbsonline.com
Email: slbs@slbsonline.com
Special Products: Academic Books and Textbooks, Fiction and Nonfiction, How-to, Linguistics, Self-help, Social Sciences, Spanish-Language Literature
Has Publisher Exclusivity:
Ariel, Crítica, Nowtilus Editores, Grupo Noriega-Limusa
Catalog Description: Children's books, General Interest and Academic Books
Titles Stocked: 300
Special Services: Cataloguing and MARC Records, Online Catalog and Online Order Processing, Order Consolidation, Pre-

approval Plans, Standing Orders, Tracking and Localization of Obscure References

Spanish Speaking Bookstore Distributions
4441 N. Broadway
Chicago, IL 60640-5659
Phone: 800-883-2126
Fax: 773-878-0647
Website: www.spanishbookstore.com
Email: ventas@spanishBookstore.com
Special Products: Religion
Catalog Description: Bilingual catalog available
Titles Stocked: 8,000
Special Services: Special Orders

SpanQuest Book Group, Inc.
6960 Camino Maquiladora St.
San Diego, CA 92154
Phone: 866-772-6783
Fax: 619-661-9958
Website: www.spanquest.com
Email: info@spanquest.com

T. R. Books
822 N. Walnut Ave.
New Braunfels, TX 78130
Phone: 830-625-2665
Fax: 830-620-0470
Website: www.trbooks.com
Email: trbooks@trbooks.com
Special Products: Nonfiction, Reference Material, Young Adult and Adult Fiction
Catalog Description: México and Latin American Publishers
Titles Stocked: 5,000
Special Services: Locate materials upon request

Technology and Education Resources Alvarez
820 North 3rd St., Suite A
Kingsville, TX 78363-4446
Phone: 361-595-0303
Fax: 361-595-4303
Website: www.tyera.com
Email: xavier@tyera.com
Special Products: ESL, GED, Movies (Spanish, Westerns), Parental Involvement, Trade, Vocational

Catalog Description: General
Titles Stocked: 3,000

Thomson Gale
27500 Drake Rd.
Farmington Hills, MI 48331-3535
Phone: 800-877-4253
Fax: 248-699-8064
Website: www.gale.com
Email: lauri.taylor@thomson.com
Special Products: Arts, Biography,
Geography, History, Language, Medicine,
Phenomena, Reference Works, Religion,
Science
Has Publisher Exclusivity: Océano Group
Catalog Description: Gale 2003 Spanish
Language Catalog
Titles Stocked: 86

Trucatriche
3800 Main St., Suite 8
Chula Vista, CA 91911
Phone: 619-426-2690
Fax: 619-426-2695
Website: www.trucatriche.com
Email: info@trucatriche.com
Special Products: Art and Culture,
Children's Books
Has Publisher Exclusivity: Artes de México,
Editorial RM, Editorial Gustavo Gili, Clio,
and Museo Tamayo
Titles Stocked: 750

Vanguard Cinema
1901 Newport Blvd., Suite 225
Costa Mesa, CA 92627
Phone: 949-258-2000
Fax: 949-258-2010
Website: www.vanguardcinema.com
Email: pgale@vanguardcinema.com
Special Products: Latino Films, U.S.
Independent Films
Has Publisher Exclusivity: Exclusive
distribution rights to all titles in catalog
Titles Stocked: 75

Versal Editorial Group, Inc.
10 High St.
Andover, MA 01810
Phone: 978-470-1972

Fax: 978-470-3812
Website: www.versalgroup.com
Email: RigoAguirre@versalgroup.com
Special Products:
Cuban Literature, Latin America Literature
Titles Stocked: 520

Vientos Tropicales
4823 Meadow Dr., Suite 103
Durham, NC 27713
Phone: 800-334-4993
Fax: 919-361-2597
Website: www.vientos.com
Email: vientos@vnet.net
Special Products: Newest Titles from Central
America
Catalog Description: Catalogs include
bibliographic information in Spanish
Titles Stocked: 5,000
Special Services: Approval Orders, Blanket
Orders, Standing Orders, US MARC Records

Weston Woods Studios
143 Main St.
Norwalk, CT 06851
Phone: 800-243-5020
Fax: 203-845-0498
Website: www.scholastic.com/westonwoods
Email: lcorra@scholastic.com
Special Products: Book/Readalong Audio
Packages, CD-ROMs, Children's Videos, DVDs
Catalog Description: Spanish Translations of
Classic Children's Literature adapted in the
Audiovisual Media
Titles Stocked: 52
Special Services: Cataloguing and Processing
Available

World of Reading, Ltd.
PO Box 13092
Atlanta, GA 30324-0092
Phone: 800-729-3703
Fax: 404-237-5511
Website: www.wor.com
Email: polyglot@wor.com
Special Products: Audio CDs/Cassettes,
Books, DVDs, Spanish Software, Videos
Titles Stocked: 800
Special Services: In-service Training for
Software.

Xenon Pictures
1440 9th St.
Santa Monica, CA 90401
Phone: 310-451-5510
Fax: 310-395-4058
Website: xenonpictures.com
Email: sales@xenonpictures.com
Special Products: Televisa Home Video VHS
and DVDs
Has Publisher Exclusivity: Televisa Home
Video
Catalog Description: Spanish-language VHS
and DVDs, including Classic TV
Programming
Titles Stocked: 25

Yoyo USA, Inc.
20326 NE 16th Place
North Miami Beach, FL 33179
Phone: 305-652-1444
Fax: 305-652-1334
Website: www.yoyousa.com
Email: info@yoyousa.com
Special Products: Children's Books, Self-help
Titles Stocked: 200

Publishers

Active Parenting Publishers
1955 Vaughn Rd. NW, Suite 108
Kennesaw, GA 30144-7808
Phone: 800-825-0060
Fax: 770-429-0334
Website: www.activeparenting.com
Email: cservice@activeparenting.com
Specialty Subjects: Parenting
U.S. Warehouse
U.S. Sales: 98%
Founded 1983 in USA
Top Authors: Betsy Gard, Ph.D., Marilyn
Montgomery, Ph.D., Michael H. Popkin,
Ph.D.

Advanced Marketing, S.A. de R.L. de C.V.
Aztecas #33, Col. Sta. Cruz Acatlán
Naucalpan, 53150, México
Phone: 52-55-5360-3139
Fax: 52-55-5360-5851
Website: www.advmkt.com
Email: carlosl@advmkt.com
Specialty Subjects: Art, Children's Books,
Cookbooks
U.S. Warehouse
Distributors: Publishers Group West
U.S. Sales: 15%
Founded 1982 in USA
Top Authors: Denis Schatz

Alfaomega Grupo Editor
Pitágoras 1139, Col. Del Valle
México City, México
Phone: 52-5575-5022
Fax: 52-5575-2490
Website: www.alfaomega.com.mx
Email: hector.german@alfaomega.com.mx
Founded 1962 in México

Aliform Publishing
117 Warwick St. SE
Minneapolis, MN 55414
Phone: 612-379-7639
Fax: 612-379-7639
Website: www.aliformgroup.com

Email: information@aliformgroup.com
Specialty Subjects: Latin American
Literature, World Literature
U.S. Warehouse
Distributors: Baker & Taylor, The
Distributors
U.S. Sales: 95%
Founded 2000 in USA
Top Authors: Eduardo García Aguilar, Joao
de Melo, Katherine Vaz

AM Editores S.A. de C.V.
Paseo de Tamarindos 400-B Suite 102, Col.
Bosques de las Lomas
México City, 05120, México
Phone: 52-55-5258-0279
Fax: 52-55-5258-0556
Website: www.ameditores.com
Email: jalegria@ameditores.com
Specialty Subjects: Architecture and Interior
Design, Cookbooks
U.S. Sales: 6%
Founded 1997 in México
Top Authors:
Chef Mónica Patiño

Amaroma Ediciones
Av. Union 266-302
Col. Americana
Guadalajara, 44160, México
Phone: 52-33-3616-5343
Fax: 52-33-3616-5346
Email: amaroma@vinet.com.mx
Specialty Subjects: Architecture, Arts and
Crafts
U.S. Warehouse
Distributors: Sunbelt Publications
U.S. Sales: 5%
Founded 1992 in México
Top Authors: Alicia Aldrete, Gutierre Aceves,
Raúl Aceves

American Academy of Pediatrics
141 Northwest Point Blvd.
Elk Grove Village, IL 60007

Phone: 888-227-1770
Fax: 847-228-1281
Website: www.aap.org/bookstore
Email: pubs@aap.org
Specialty Subjects: Health, Parenting
U.S. Warehouse
Distributors: Baker & Taylor, JA Majors
U.S. Sales: 10%
Founded 1929 in USA
Top Authors: Robert E. Hannemann, MD,
FAAP; Steven P. Shelov, MD, FAAP

Angel Editor
Dr. Lucio 103-A3-L2.1
México City, México
Phone: 52-55-5761-4589
Fax: 52-55-5761-4589
Website: www.angeleditor.com
Email: info@angeleditor.com
Specialty Subjects: Law
Imprints: Enciclopedia Jurídica Omeba
Founded 1995 in México
Top Authors: Bernardo Feijóo, Cancio Meliá,
Gunther Jakobs

Anglo Didáctica Publishing
Santiago de Compostela 16,
Piso Bajo, Letra B
Madrid, 28034, Spain
Phone: 34-91-378-0188
Fax: 34-91-378-0188
Email: librosdeingles@tiscali.es
Specialty Subjects: Learning Foreign
Languages
Distributors: The Bilingual Publications
Company, Books on Wings/Brodart,
Lectorum Publications
U.S. Sales: 20%
Founded 1986 in Spain
Top Authors:
Ana Merino, Peter Rutherford, Susan Taylor

Another Language Press
7709 Hamilton Ave
Cincinnati, OH 45231
Phone: 513-521-5590
Fax: 513-521-5592
Website: www.aimsbooks.com
Email: aimsbooks@fuse.net
Specialty Subjects: Children's Books

U.S. Warehouse
Distributors: Aims International Books
Founded 1990 in USA

Arco Libros, S. L.
c/Juan Bautista de Toledo 28
Madrid, 28002, Spain
Phone: 34-91-415-3687
Fax: 34-91-413-5907
Website: www.arcomuralla.com
Email: arcolibros@arcomuralla.com
Specialty Subjects: History, Library Science,
Spanish as a Foreign Language
U.S. Sales: 3%
Founded 1984 in Spain
Top Authors:
Julián Martín Abad, Leonardo Gómez
Torrego, Manuel Alavar Ezquerra

Arte Público Press
University of Houston, 452
Cullen Performance Hall
Houston, TX 77204-2004
Phone: 713-743-2999
Fax: 713-743-3080
Website: www.artepublicopress.com
Email: mparle@central.uh.edu
Imprints: Piñata Books
U.S. Warehouse
Distributors: All Major Distributors, Baker
& Taylor, Ingram, Lectorum
U.S. Sales: 99%
Founded 1979 in USA
Top Authors: Judith Ortiz Cofer, Nicholasa
Mohr, Pat Mora, Victor Villaseñor

Artes de México y del Mundo, S.A. de C.V.
Cordoba 69, Col. Roma
México D.F., 06700, México
Phone: 52-55-25-4036
Fax: 52-55-25-5925
Website: www.artesdemexico.com
Email: artesdeMéxico@artesdemexico.com
Specialty Subjects: Architecture, Art and
Photography, Cultural Expressions, Popular Art
Distributors: Trucatriche
U.S. Sales: 10%
Founded 1953 in México
Top Authors: Alfredo López Austin, Miguel
León Portilla, Octavio Paz

Asunto Impreso
Pasaje Rivarola, 169
Buenos Aires, Argentina
Phone: 54-11-4-383-6262
Fax: 54-11-4-383-5152
Website: www.asuntoimpreso.com
Email: www@asuntoimpreso.com
Specialty Subjects: Art
Distributors: DAP
U.S. Sales: 2%
Founded 1995 in Argentina
Top Authors:
Alfredo Benavides Bedoya, Daniel Santoro,
Santiago Melazzini

B. Jain Publishers Overseas
1920 10th St., Chuna Mandi, Pahar Ganj
New Delhi, 110055, India
Phone: 91-11-2356-2572
Fax: 91-11-2358-0471
Website: www.bjainbooks.com
Email: bjain@vsnl.com
Specialty Subjects: Homeopathy Medical
Books
U.S. Sales: 15%
Founded 1971 in India
Top Authors:
Clarke, Hehnemann, Kent

Barefoot Books
2067 Massachusetts Ave.
Cambridge, MA 02140
Phone: 617-576-0660
Fax: 617-576-0049
Website: www.barefootbooks.com
Email: ussales@barefootbooks.com
Specialty Subjects: Multicultural children's
books
U.S. Warehouse
Distributors: Baker & Taylor, Book
Wholesalers Inc., Follett, Ingram
U.S. Sales: 70%
Founded 1993 in United Kingdom
Top Authors: Mary Finch, Mary-Joan
Gerson, Stella Blackstone

Barnhardt & Ashe Publishing, Inc.
Suite 51, PMB 432
Miami, FL 33131
Phone: 410-707-6686

Fax: 305-545-0106
Email: BarnhardtAshe@aol.com
Specialty Subjects: Children's Books, Fiction,
Poetry, Scholarly Publications
Imprints: Belles Enfants
U.S. Warehouse
U.S. Sales: 100%
Founded 2001 in USA
Top Authors: Charles Charlton, Kathleen L.
Davis, Sharon Belle

Beatriz Viterbo Editora
España 1150
Rosario, S2000DBX, Argentina
Phone: 54-341-4487521/4827560
Fax: 54-341-4261919
Website: www.beatrizviterbo.com.ar
Email: info@beatrizviterbo.com.ar
Specialty Subjects: Argentine Literature,
Cultural Studies, Fiction, Latin American
Literature, Literary Reviews
Distributors: Amazon, Latin American Book
Source, Latin American Book Store
U.S. Sales: 10%
Founded 1991 in Argentina
Top Authors:
César Aira, Ezequiel Martínez Estrada,
Manuel Puig

Berbera Editores, S.A. de C.V.
Delibes 96, Col. Guadalupe Victoria
México City, 07790, México
Phone: 52-55-5356-4405
Fax: 52-55-5356-6599
Website: www.berbera.com.mx
Email: editores@berbera.com.mx
Specialty Subjects: Esoteric, Religion, Self-
help
Distributors: Bernard H. Hamel Spanish
Book Distributors, Lectorum
U.S. Sales: 5%
Founded 1990 in México
Top Authors: Armando Cosani, H.P.
Blavatsky, J.M. Ragón

Berklee Press
1140 Boylston St.
Boston, MA 02215
Phone: 866-237-5533
Fax: 617-747-2149

Website: www.berkleepress.com
Email: info@berkleepress.com
Specialty Subjects: Instructional Music
Books, Instructional Music DVDs
U.S. Warehouse
Distributors: Hal Leonard
U.S. Sales: 100%
Founded 1958 in USA
Top Authors: Matt Marvuglio, Stephen
Webber, William Leavitt

Bernan Press
4611–F Assembly Dr.
Lanham, MD 20706-4391
Phone: 800-865-3457
Fax: 800-865-3450
Website: www.bernan.com
Email: info@bernan.com
Specialty Subjects: Government Information,
Reference
U.S. Warehouse
Founded 1992 in USA

Bilingual Books, Inc.
1719 West Nickerson St.
Seattle, WA 98119
Phone: 800-488-5068
Fax: 206-284-3660
Website: www.bbks.com
Email: info@bbks.com
Specialty Subjects: Audio CD Titles, ESL
Instruction Books, Phrase Guides, Spanish
Instruction Books
U.S. Warehouse
Distributors: Baker & Taylor, Ingram, West
Book Distributing Inc.
Founded 1981 in USA

Bilingual Review Press
Hispanic Research Center
Arizona State University
PO Box 872702
Tempe, AZ 85287-2702
Phone: 480-965-3867
Fax: 480-965-8309
Website: www.asu.edu/brp
Email: brp@asu.edu
Specialty Subjects: Literary Works by U.S.
Latinos, Scholarly Works
U.S. Warehouse

Distributors: Baker & Taylor, Brodart,
Ingram, Small Press Distribution
U.S. Sales: 99%
Founded 1973 in USA
Top Authors: Ana Castillo, Elva Treviño
Hart, Rolando Hinojosa

Blue Mountain Arts, Inc.
1512 East Broward Blvd., Suite 300
Fort Lauderdale, FL 33301
Phone: 954-522-0055
Fax: 954-522-5330
Website: www.sps.com
Email: booksbma@mindspring.com
Specialty Subjects: Family, Gift, Inspiration,
Self-help, Spiritual, Teen
Imprints: Blue Mountain Press, Rabbit's Foot
Press
U.S. Warehouse
Distributors: Baker & Taylor, Ingram, Koen
Founded 1971 in USA
Top Authors: Ashley Rice, Douglas Pagels,
Susan Polis Schutz

Bonus Books
1223 Wilshire Blvd., PO Box 597
Santa Monica, CA 90403
Phone: 310-260-9400
Fax: 310-260-9494
Website: www.bonusbooks.com
Email: Stephanie@bonusbooks.com
Specialty Subjects: Christian Books, Fiction,
How-to, Nonfiction, Pop Culture
Imprints: Bonus Books, True Ink, Volt Press
U.S. Warehouse
Distributors: National Book Network
Founded in USA

Bridge Publications
4751 Fountain Ave.
Los Angeles, CA 90029
Phone: 323-953-3320
Fax: 323-953-3328
Website: www.bridgepub.com
Email: info@bridgepub.com
Specialty Subjects: Health and Fitness,
Religion, Self-help, Spirituality
U.S. Warehouse
Distributors: Baker & Taylor, Ingram
U.S. Sales: 95%

Founded 1981 in USA
Top Authors: L. Ron Hubbard

Broadman & Holman Publishers
127 9th Ave. N
Nashville, TN 37234
Phone: 800-251-3225
Fax: 615-251-2469
Website: www.broadmanholman.com
Specialty Subjects: Bibles, Biblical
References, Inspirational, Religion
Imprints: B & H Español
U.S. Warehouse
Distributors: Baker & Taylor, Ingram
Founded 1801 in USA
Top Authors: Beth Moore, Jerry Jenkins, Tim
LaHayes

Brosquil Ediciones
Plaza Pintor Segrelles, 1 Esc.
B Pta. 25
Madrid, Spain
Phone: 34-96-310-7045
Fax: 34-96-341-8341
Website: www.brosquilediciones.es
Email: brosquilediciones@hotmail.com
Specialty Subjects: Children's and Young
Adult Titles, Novels
Distributors: Lectorum
U.S. Sales: 1%
Founded 2000 in Spain
Top Authors:
Carles Arbat, Manel Alonso I Catala, Marta
Rivera Ferner

Buenas Letras/Rosen Publishing
29 East 21st St.
New York, NY 10010
Phone: 212-777-3017
Fax: 888-436-4643
Website: www.buenasletras.com
Email: Mauriciov@rosenpub.com
Specialty Subjects: Curriculum-related and
high-interest books for children and young
adults, pre-K to 12th grade. Spanish-language
and bilingual titles. American History,
Science, Sports, Technology, Health, Social
Studies, Cultural Diversity, Biography
Imprints: Editorial Buenas Letras, PowerKids
Press, PowerPlus, PowerStart Press, Rosen

Central, Rosen Publishing
U.S. Warehouse
Founded 1950 in USA

Bull Publishing
PO Box 1377
Boulder, CO 80306
Phone: 800-676-2855
Specialty Subjects: Medical, Nutrition, Self-
help, Sports Medicine
Distributors: Publishers Group West
U.S. Sales: 90%
Founded 1973 in USA
Top Authors: Deborah Stewart, Kate Lorig

Cantemos
15696 Altamira Dr.
Chino Hills, CA 91709
Phone: 800-393-1336
Fax: 909-393-1362
Websites:
www.cantemosco.com and
www.simplespanishsongs.com
Email: jarjetb@aol.com
Specialty Subjects: Songs in Spanish from
Latin America
U.S. Warehouse
Distributors: Baker & Taylor, Follet Library
Resources
U.S. Sales: 100%
Founded 1991 in USA
Top Authors: Michael Mastorakis

Capstone Press
151 Good Counsel Dr.
Mankato, MN 56002-0669
Phone: 800-747-4992
Fax: 888-262-0705
Website: www.capstonepress.com
Specialty Subjects: Children's Nonfiction
Imprints: A+ Books, Bridgestone Books,
Edge Books, Fact Finders, First Facts, Pebble
Books, Pebble Plus
U.S. Warehouse
Distributors: Baker & Taylor, Delaney
Educational Enterprises, DLB Educational
Corporation, Follet, Garrett Book Company,
Hertzberg-New Method, National
Educational Systems, Rainbow Book
Company

U.S. Sales: 95%
Top Authors:
Adele Richardson, Helen Frost, Lola Schaefer

Caribe Betania Editories (Thomas Nelson Publishing)
501 Nelson Place
Nashville, TN 37214
Phone: 615-902-1890
Fax: 615-883-9376
Website: www.caribebetania.com
Email: srodriguez@thomasnelson.com
Specialty Subjects: Family Issues, Inspirational, Leadership, Self-help
Imprints: Thomas Nelson, Tommy Nelson, W Publishing
U.S. Warehouse
Distributors: DCI Int'l, Pan de Vida
U.S. Sales: 67%
Founded 1949 in Costa Rica
Founded 1991 in USA
Top Authors: John Maxwell, Max Lucado

Carroggio, S.A. de Ediciones
c/Pelai, 28-30, 4
Barcelona, 08001, Spain
Phone: 34-93-494-9922
Fax: 34-93-494-9923
Website: www.carroggio.com
Email: editorial@carroggio.es
Specialty Subjects: Art, Dictionaries, Encyclopedias, Geography, History, Reference
Founded 1911 in Spain
Top Authors:
Fernández Alvarez, Javier Tusell, LM Enciso

Casa Creación
600 Rinehart Rd.
Lake Mary, FL 32746
Phone: 407-333-7117
Fax: 407-333-7147
Website: www.casacreacion.com
Email: casacreacion@strang.com
Specialty Subjects: Children's Books, Christian Music, Inspirational Books
Imprints: Casa Creación, Casa Kids, Iglesia Para Niños
U.S. Warehouse
Distributors: Anderson News, Ingram, Pan de Vida

U.S. Sales: 50%
Founded 1997 in USA
Top Authors: John Maxwell, Joyce Meyer, Max Lucado

Cato Institute
1000 Massachusetts Ave.
Washington, DC 20001
Phone: 202-842-0200
Fax: 202-842-0779
Websites: www.elcato.org (Spanish language) or www.cato.org
Email: books@cato.org
Specialty Subjects: Economics, Foreign Policy, Public Policy
U.S. Warehouse
Distributors: National Book Network
U.S. Sales: 95%
Founded 1977 in USA
Top Authors: Patrick Michaels

Celya Editorial
Apartado Postal 102
Salamanca, 37080, Spain
Phone: 34-63-9542-794
Fax: 34-92-3271-945
Website: www.editorialcelya.com
Email: celya@editorialcelya.com
Specialty Subjects: Literature
Founded 1999 in Spain
Top Authors:
Antonio Colinas, Care Santos, Victoriano Cremér

Centro de Investigaciones y Publicaciones
Apartado 441
Lima, 100, Peru
Phone: 511-423-2772
Fax: 511-423-2772
Email: mariaesther59@hotmail.com
Specialty Subjects: Christian Books.
Founded 1992 in Peru

Certeza Argentina
Bernardo de Irigoyen 654
Buenos Aires, C1072AAC, Argentina
Phone: 4331-6651
Fax: 4334-8278
Website: www.libreriacerteza.com.ar
Email: certeza@certezaargentina.com.ar

Specialty Subjects: Religion
U.S. Warehouse
Distributors: Christian Internacional,
Luciano, Pan de Vida, Visión Joven
Founded 1968 in Argentina
Top Authors:
John Stot, John White, Lucas Leys

Chelsea Green Publishing Co.
85 North Main St.
White River Jct., VT 05001
Phone: 802-295-6300 ext 106
Fax: 802-295-6444
Website: www.chelseagreen.com
Email: blackmer@chelseagreen.com
Specialty Subjects: Food, Nature
U.S. Warehouse
U.S. Sales: 20%
Founded 1984 in USA
Top Authors: Julia Alvarez

Children's Book Press
2211 Mission St.
San Francisco, CA 94110
Phone: 415-821-3080
Fax: 415-821-3081
Website: www.childrensbookpress.org
Email: info@childrensbookpress.org
Specialty Subjects: Children's Books
U.S. Warehouse
Distributors: Publishers Group West
U.S. Sales: 90%
Founded 1975 in USA
Top Authors: Carmen Lomas Garza,
Francisco Alarcón, Juan Felipe Herrera

**Children's Press (Scholastic Library
Publishing)**
90 Old Sherman Turnpike
Danbury, CT 06816
Phone: 800-621-1115
Fax: 866-783-4361
Website: www.scholastic.com/
librarypublishing
Email: sjames@scholasticlibrary.com
Specialty Subjects: Children's Books
Imprints: Childrens Press, Franklin Watts,
Grolier, Grolier Online
Founded in USA
U.S. Warehouse

Chronicle Books, LLC
85 Second St., 6th Floor
San Francisco, CA 94105
Phone: 415-537-4200
Fax: 415-537-4460
Website: www.chroniclebooks.com
Email: frontdesk@chroniclebooks.com
Specialty Subjects: Architecture, Art,
Children's Books, Design, Food, Lifestyle,
Photography, Pop Culture
U.S. Warehouse
Distributors: Front St., Handprint Books,
Innovative Kids, North-South Books,
Princeton Architectural Press, Ragged Bears
Publishing
Founded 1966 in USA

Cidcli
Ave. México 145, Oficina 601
México City, México
Phone: 5255-5659-7524
Fax: 5255-5659-3186
Website: www.cidcli.com.mx
Email: cidcli@att.net.mx
Specialty Subjects: Children's and Young
Adult Books
Distributors: Aims, Books on Wings,
Mariuccia Iaconi Books, Lectorum, Libros
Sin Fronteras.
U.S. Sales: 30%
Founded 1980 in México
Top Authors: Alonso Nóñez, Felipe Garrido,
Fernando del Paso

Cie Inversiones Editoriales Dossat 2000 S.L.
Avenida Pio Xii, 57, Portal A
Madrid, 28016, Spain
Phone: 34-91-359-1090
Fax: 34-91-350-9381
Website: www.ciedossat.com
Email: comercial@ciedossat.com
Specialty Subjects: Automotive,
Construction, Cookbooks, Humanities,
Management, Urban Planning
Distributors: Celesa
U.S. Sales: 2%
Founded 1886 in Spain
Top Authors:
David Suriol, Enrique Rojas, Manuel Arias-Paz

Cinco Puntos Press
701 Texas Ave
El Paso, TX 79901
Phone: 800-566-9072
Fax: 915-838-1635
Website: www.cincopuntos.com
Email: info@cincopuntos.com
Specialty Subjects: Bilingual Children's
Books; Fiction, Non-Fiction, and Poetry from
the U.S. México Border, México and the U.S.
Southwest
Distributors: Consortium Book Sales and
Distribution
U.S. Sales: 98%
Founded 1985 in USA
Top Authors: Benjamin Alire Sáenz, Joe
Hayes, Luis Albert Urrea, Paco Ignacio Taibo,
Subcomandante Marcos

Clear Light Publishing Corp.
823 Don Diego
Santa Fe, NM 87505
Phone: 505-989-9590
Fax: 505-989-9519
Website: www.clearlightbooks.com
Email: publish@clearlightbooks.com
Specialty Subjects: Spanish and Bilingual
Children's Books, Cookbooks, Hispanic Art
and Culture, Native American Art and
Culture, Tibetan Art and Culture
U.S. Warehouse
Distributors: All Trade Distributors, Clear
Light Distribution, Ingram.
U.S. Sales: 95%
Founded 1980 in USA

Cocolo Editorial
Calle Santiago # 115
Santo Domingo, Dominican Republic
Phone: 808-685-0589
Fax: 809-689-3195
Email: avelinostanley@hotmail.com
Specialty Subjects: Literature
Distributors: Calíope Bookstore, Lectorum,
Tópoka Bookstore
U.S. Sales: 20%
Founded 1994 in Dominican Republic
Top Authors: Avelino Stanley, Minelys
Sánchez, Pablo Armando Fernández

Combel Editorial, S.A.
c/Caspe 79 08013
Barcelona, Spain
Phone: 34-93-244-95-50
Fax: 34-93-265-68-95
Website: www.editorialcasals.com
Email: combel@editorialcasals.com
Founded 1986 in Spain
Top Authors:
Patricia Geis, Ricardo Alcantara

Consultores en Ciencias Humanas, S.L.
Zubileta, 16 Local 48
903 Burceña
Baracaldo, Spain
Phone: 34-94-485-0497
Fax: 34-94-485-0122
Website: www.grupoalbor-cohs.com
Email: editor@grupoalbor-cohs.com
Specialty Subjects: Psychological and
Educational Resources
U.S. Warehouse
U.S. Sales: 3%
Founded 1995 in Spain
Top Authors: Ángela Magaz Lago, Emanuel
García Pérez, Manuel Toro

**Creative Publishing International
/Two-Can Publishing**
18705 Lake Dr. East
Chanhassen, MN 55317
Phone: 800-328-0590
Fax: 952-988-0201
Website: www.creativepub.com
Email: sales@creativepub.com
Specialty Subjects: Children's Books, How-
to, Nature and Wildlife, Photography
Imprints: NorthWord Books for Young
Readers, NorthWord Press, Two-Can
Publishing
U.S. Warehouse
Distributors: Baker & Taylor, Ingram
U.S. Sales: 5%
Founded 1969 in USA

Curbstone Press
321 Jackson St.
Willimantic, CT 06226
Phone: 860-423-5110
Fax: 860-423-9242

Website: www.curbstone.org
Email: info@curbstone.org
Specialty Subjects: Fiction, Literature, Poetry
U.S. Warehouse
U.S. Sales: 95%
Founded 1975 in USA
Top Authors: Claribel Alegría, Louis J.
Rodriguez, Miguel Barnet

CWD México, S.A. de C.V.
Juan Kepler 4047, Col. Arboledas
Zapopán, 45070, México
Phone: 52-33-3809-5754
Fax: 52-55-5554-3215
Website: www.cwdmexico.com
Email: aramirez@cwdmexico.com
Specialty Subjects: Educational CD-ROMs
U.S. Sales: 2%
Founded 1998 in México

de Dios Editores
Cerrito 1222
Buenos Aires, 1010, Argentina
Phone: 54-11-481-63514
Fax: 541-1-4-816-3514
Website: www.dediosonline.com
Email: info@dediosonline.com
Specialty Subjects: Entertainment, Tourism
U.S. Warehouse
Distributors: Treaty Oak Map Distributor
Founded 1993 in Argentina
Top Authors: Horacio de Dios

Desclée de Brouwer, S.A.
Henao, 6, 3 Derecha
Barcelona, Spain
Phone: 34-94-423-3045
Fax: 34-94-423-7594
Website: www.edesclee.com
Email: info@edesclee.com
Specialty Subjects: Psychology, Religion,
Self-help
Distributors: Saint Paul Distribution Center,
SBD Books
U.S. Sales: 10%
Founded 1944 in Spain
Top Authors: Albert Ellis, José María
Castillo, Olga Castanyer

**Distribuidora de Publicaciones Oveja
Negra, Ltda.**
Transv. 93 # 62–46
Interior 16
Bogotá, Colombia
Phone: 571-252-9694
Fax: 571-434-4139
Website: www.distovejanegra.com
Email: dipon@andinet.com
Specialty Subjects: Children and Young
Adult, Contemporary Literature, Economics,
General Interest, Politics
Imprints: Editorial Oveja Negra, Indigo
Ediciones
U.S. Sales: 3%
Founded 1992 in Colombia
Top Authors: David Cherician

Distribuidora Lewis S.A.
PO Box 0816-06733, Zone 5
Panama City, Panama
Phone: 507-212-1888
Fax: 507-212-1450
Website: www.distribuidoralewis.com
Email: info@distribuidoralewis.com
Specialty Subjects: Novels, Readers,
Textbooks.
Distributors: Lectorum, SBD Spanish Book
Distributors, The Bilingual Publications
Founded 1925 in Panama
Top Authors: Dalys de Bazan, Eneida
Quezada de Walton, Noris Correa de Sanjur

Distribuidora Norma, Inc.
P.O. Box 195040
San Juan, PR 00919-5040
Phone: 800-BOOKS-58
Fax: 787-788-7161
Website: www.norma.com
Email: uroldan@normapr.com
Specialty Subjects: Business and Commerce,
Children and Young Adult Literature, Health
and Family, Reference and Dictionaries, Self-
help, Textbooks
Imprints: Belaqua, Farben, Granica,
Greenwich, Kapeluz, Parramón, Voluntad
U.S. Warehouse
Distributors: All Major U.S. Distributors
Founded 1960 in Colombia

Top Authors: Carlos Alberto Montaner, Gabriel García Márquez, Walter Riso

DK Publishing
375 Hudson St., 2nd Floor
New York, NY 10014
Phone: 212-213-4800
Fax: 212-689-4828
Website: www.dk.com
Email: kim@highland@dk.com
Specialty Subjects: Child Care, Children's Nonfiction, Entertainment, Gardening, Health, History, Reference, Self-help, Travel
U.S. Warehouse
U.S. Sales: 50%
Founded 1974 in United Kingdom
Top Authors: Peter Ackroyd, Rick Smollan, Tom Peters

Dolo Publications, Inc.
12800 Briar Forest Dr., #23
Houston, TX 77077
Phone: 281-493-4552
Fax: 281-679-9092
Website: www.dololanguages.com
Email: dolo@wt.net
Specialty Subjects: Instructional Books for the Study of Foreign Languages and ESL, many with CDs
Distributors: Carlex, Delta Systems, Teacher's Discovery
Founded 1985 in USA

Dominie Press
1949 Kellogg Ave.
Carlsbad, CA 92008
Phone: 760-431-8000
Fax: 760-431-8777
Website: www.dominie.com
Email: yun@dominie.com
Specialty Subjects: Publishers of English and Spanish K–8 Supplementary Reading
Founded 1975 in USA

Downtown Book Center
247 SE 1st St.
Miami, FL 33131
Phone: 305-377-9941
Fax: 305-371-5926

Website: yp.bellsouth.com/sites/downtownbooks/
Email: raxdown@aol.com
Specialty Subjects: Cuba-Related Themes, Cuban Cookbooks
Imprints: Dax Books
U.S. Warehouse
Distributors: Downtown Book Center, Spanish Periodicals
Founded 1965 in USA

Early Advantage
79 Sanford St.
Fairfield, CT 06824
Phone: 888-327-5923
Fax: 800-409-9928
Website: www.early-advantage.com
Email: lynnj@early-advantage.com
Specialty Subjects: ESL, Foreign Language, History, Language Arts, Music
U.S. Warehouse
Founded in USA

Edelvives
c/Xaudaró # 25
Madrid, 28034, Spain
Phone: 34-91-334-4883
Fax: 34-91-334-4893
Website: www.edelvives.es
Email: rmarmol@edelvives.es
Specialty Subjects: Children and Young Adult Literature, Textbooks
Imprints: Alhucema, Baula, Edelvives, Ibaizabal, Tambre
Founded 1890 in Spain
Top Authors:
Gonzalo Moure, Joan Manuel Gisbert, Ricardo Gómez

Edere
Mérida 65, Col. Roma
México City, 06700, México
Phone: 52-55-5514-7769
Fax: 52-55-5514-7770
Email: edit_edere@yahoo.com
Founded in México

Edibesa
Calle Madre de Dios, 35
Madrid, 28016, Spain

Phone: 34-91-345-1992
Fax: 34-91-350-5099
Website: www.edibesa.com
Email: edibesa@planalfa.es
Specialty Subjects: Religion
U.S. Sales: 5%
Founded 1984 in Spain
Top Authors: François Mauriac, José María
Pemán, Juan Pablo II

Ediciones 2010
Paseo de la Castellana, 100, 2B
Madrid, Spain
Phone: 34-91-564-9324
Fax: 34-91-563-8400
Website: www.ediciones2010.com
Email: marketing@ediciones2010.com
Specialty Subjects: Business and Economics,
Social Sciences
U.S. Sales: 3%
Founded 1996 in Spain
Top Authors:
Enrique Fuentes-Quintana, Juan Velarde,
Ramón Tamames

Ediciones Alfar, S.A.
Polígono Industrial La Chaparrilla
Parcela 36
Cta. Sevilla-Málaga, Km. 3
41016, Spain
Phone: 34-95-440-6100
Fax: 34-95-440-2580
Website: www.edalfar.es.vg
Email: alfaraa@teleline.es
Specialty Subjects: History, Humanities and
Philosophy, Literature
Founded 1982 in Spain
Top Authors: Manuel Ángel Vázquez Medel,
Manuel Moreno Alonso

Ediciones Arq
Los Navegantes 1963, Providencia
Santiago, Chile
Phone: 562-686-5630
Fax: 562-686-5634
Website: www.puc.cl/edicionesarq
Email: arqedic@puc.cl
Specialty Subjects: Architecture and Design
Distributors: Howard Karno Books, Inc.
U.S. Sales: 10%

Founded 1990 in Chile
Top Authors: Alejandro Aravena Mori,
Fernando Pérez Oyarzun, Rodrigo Pérez de
Arce

Ediciones B
Bradley # 52, Col. Anzures
México City, 11590, México
Phone: 52-55-1101-0662
Fax: 52-55-5254-2067
Website: www.edicionesb-america.com
Email: nrufrancos@edicionesb.com
Specialty Subjects: Children and Young
Adult, Literature, Self-help
Imprints: Ediciones B, Salo, Vergara
Distributors: Distal, Girón Books, Mariuccia
Iaconi Books, Lectorum, Libros Sin Fronteras
U.S. Sales: 7%
Founded 1987 in Spain
Top Authors: Brian Weiss, Gerardo Reyes,
John Grisham

Ediciones Callejón, Inc.
Avenida Las Palmas, 1108, Pda. 18
San Juan, PR 00908-0024
Phone: 787-723-8566
Fax: 787-723-5850
Email: edicionescallejon@yahoo.com
Specialty Subjects: Essays, Literature
U.S. Warehouse
Distributors: Amazon, Exodus
U.S. Sales: 20%
Founded 1999 in Puerto Rico
Top Authors: Arcadio Diaz Quiñonez, Mayra
Montero, Rafael Acevedo

Ediciones Castillo
Privada Francisco L. Rocha, 7
Col. San Jeronimo
Monterrey, 64630, México
Phone: 52-81-8347-6215
Fax: 52-81-8333-2804
Website: www.edicionescastillo.com
Email: acastillo@edicionescastillo.com
Founded in México

Ediciones Colihue, S.R.L.
Ac. Diaz Velez 5125
Buenos Aires, C1405DCG, Argentina
Phone: 5411-4-958-4442

Fax: 5411-4-958-5673
Website: www.colihue.com.ar
Email: ecolihue@colihue.com.ar
Specialty Subjects: Anthropology, Architecture, Arts and Crafts, Astronomy and Science, Biographies, Dictionaries and Reference, Essays, History, Law, Nonfiction, Poetry, Pop Culture, University Textbooks, Classics
Distributors: Libros Sin Fronteras
Founded 1982 in Argentina
Top Authors: Alejandro Dolina, Graciela Montes, Leopoldo Marechal

Ediciones Crecimiento Cristiano
5903 Villa Nueva, Casilla 3
Córdoba, Argentina
Phone: 5451-353-491-1181
Website: www.edicionescc.com
Email: ecc@edicionescc.com
Specialty Subjects: Religious Books
Founded in Argentina

Ediciones Cristiandad, S.A.
c/Serrano 51, Primera izq.
Madrid, Spain
Phone: 34-91-781-9970
Fax: 34-91-781-9977
Website: www.edicionescristiandd.es
Email: info@edicionescristiandad.es
U.S. Sales: 10%
Founded 1968 in Spain
Top Authors: Karl Rahner, Romano Guardini

Ediciones Dabar, S.A. de C.V.
Mirador #42, Col. El Mirador
México City, 04950, México
Phone: 52-55-5603-3630; 5673-8855
Fax: 52-55-5603-3674
Website: www.dabar.com.mx
Email: dabar.ediciones@prodigy.net.mx
Specialty Subjects: Religion, Science Fiction, Self-help
Distributors: Distribuidora Mana, Gethesemani Librería Católica, Librería San Pablo, Sepi Book Service, Spanish Speaking Bookstore Distribution
U.S. Sales: 3%
Founded 1991 in México

Top Authors: José Luis González, Juan Bautista Libanio, Leonardo Boff

Ediciones de la Flor
Gorriti 3695
1172 Buenos Aires, Argentina
Phone: 54-11-4963-7950
Fax: 54-11-4963-5616
Website: www.edicionesdelaflor.com.ar
Email: edic-flor@datamarkets.com.ar
Specialty Subjects: Children and Young Adult, Fiction, History, Humor, Theater and Cinema
Distributors: The Bilingual Publications Co., Books on Wings/Brodart Español, Bookspan, Ideal Foreign Books, Lectorum, Mariuccia Iaconi, Pan American Books
U.S. Sales: 5%
Founded 1966 in Argentina
Top Authors: Ariel Dorfman, Luis Rafael Sánchez, Quino (Mafalda)

Ediciones del Candil
Nicaragua 4462
Buenos Aires, Argentina
Phone: 54 11 4032 8260
Fax: 54-11-4832-7980
Email: agcandil@ciudad.com.ar
Specialty Subjects: Law, Literature, Social Sciences
Founded 1998 in Argentina

Ediciones del Laberinto
c/Martínez Corrochano, 3, 2™ Planta
Madrid, Spain
Phone: 34-91-433-5752
Fax: 34-91-501-3972
Website: www.edicioneslaberinto.es
Email: laberinto@edicioneslaberinto.es
Specialty Subjects: Children and Young Adult Literature, Literary Reviews, Textbooks
Imprints: Apóstrofe, Espejo de Tinta, Laberinto
U.S. Sales: 1%
Founded 1989 in Spain
Top Authors: Concha Calleja, Henri Pena, Pedro Ortega

Ediciones Edigol
Calle San Gabriel 50
Barcelona, Spain
Phone: 34-93-372-63-04
Website: www.edigol.com
Email: info@edigol.com
Specialty Subjects: Cartography
Founded 1976 in Spain

Ediciones Ekaré
Edif. Banco del Libro
Ave. Luis Roche, Altamira
Caracas, 1062, Venezuela
Phone: 58-212-263-0091
Fax: 58-212-263-3291
Website: www.ekare.com.ve
Email: books@ekare.com.ve
Specialty Subjects: Children and Young
Adult.
U.S. Warehouse
Distributors: Aims International, Chulainn,
Donars Spanish Books, Lectorum, Libros Sin
Fronteras, Mariuccia Iaconi Book Imports,
The Bilingual Publications Co.
U.S. Sales: 46%
Founded 1978 in Venezuela
Top Authors: Antonio Skármeta, Chris Van
Allsburg, Pablo Neruda.

Ediciones Emete
Avenida Ejercito #26
Santiago, Chile
Phone: 56-696-25-12
Fax: 56-696-25-12
Email: emete@terra.cl;
edicionesemete@hotmail.com
Distributors: Amazon.com, Barnes & Noble,
xlibris.com.
U.S. Sales: 18%
Founded 1989 in Chile
Top Authors: Emilio Rojas, Mario Terrazas.

Ediciones Era, S.A. de C.V.
Calle del Trabajo, 31
Col. La Fama, Tlalpan
México City, 14269, México
Phone: 52-55-5528-1221
Fax: 52-55-5606-2904
Website: www.edicionesera.com.mx
Email: edicionesera@laneta.apc.org

Specialty Subjects: Art, Literature, Social
Sciences.
U.S. Sales: 12%
Founded 1960 in México
Top Authors: Elena Poniatowska, José Emilio
Pacheco, Sergio Pitol.

Ediciones Fiscales ISEF, S.A.
Avenida del Taller # 82
Col. Tránsito
México City, México
Phone: 52-55-5096-5100
Fax: 52-55-5096-5100
Website: www.libreriaisel.com.mx
Email: editorial@grupoisef.com.mx
Specialty Subjects: Business Management,
Finance, Fiscal and Legal Books,
International Business, Law, Self-
improvement
Founded 1973 in México
Top Authors: Andres Rohde Ponce, Dr.
Herbert Bettinger Barrios

Ediciones Jaguar
c/ Laurel 23, 1
Madrid, 28005, Spain
Phone: 34-91-474-1140
Fax: 34-91-474-4074
Website: www.edicionesjaguar.com
Email: jaguar@edicionesjaguar.com
Specialty Subjects: Art, Cinema, Health,
Self-help, Travel
Founded 1986 in Spain

Ediciones Larousse
c/o Houghton Mifflin Company
222 Berkeley St.
Boston, MA
Phone: 800-225-3362
Fax: 800-634-7568
Website: www.houghtonmifflinbooks.com
Specialty Subjects: Reference
U.S. Warehouse
Founded in México

Ediciones Lumbrera
Apartado 1631-2100
San Jose, Costa Rica
Phone: 506-253-5820
Fax: 506-253-4723

Email: edicioneslumbrera@hotmail.com
Specialty Subjects: Christian Books
Founded 1998 in Costa Rica
Top Authors: Elisel Guzmán, Ruth Mooney, Tatiana Anderson

Ediciones Lumiere, S.A.
Piedras 1675, P.B. 'A'
Buenos Aires, 1140, Argentina
Phone: 54-11-4361-0986
Fax: 54-11-4361-4541
Website: www.edicioneslumiere.com
Email: danchorena@edicioneslumiere.com
Specialty Subjects: Communications, Education, Law and History, Literature and Essays, Psychology and Sociology, Social Sciences
Imprints: Lumiere, Reflejos
Top Authors: Andrew Graham-Yooll, Raanan Rein, Ruth Sautu

Ediciones Mensajero, S.A.
c/Sancho de Azpeitia, 2 Bajo
Barcelona, Spain
Phone: 34-94-447-0358
Fax: 34-94-447-2630
Website: www.mensajero.com
Email: mensajero@mensajero.com
Specialty Subjects: Humanities, Religion
U.S. Sales: 2%
Founded 1915 in Spain
Top Authors:
Hedwig Lewis, Luis Alonso Schokel

Ediciones Morata, S.L.
c/ Mejia Lequerica, 12
Madrid, Spain
Phone: 34-91-448-0926
Fax: 34-91-448-0925
Website: www.edmorata.es
Email: morata@edmorata.es
Specialty Subjects: Pedagogy, Psychology, Social Sciences, Sociology
Distributors: The Bilingual Publications Co., Celesa, Puvill
U.S. Sales: 1%
Founded 1920 in Spain
Top Authors: Dewey, Piget

Ediciones Narcea, S.A.
Avda. Dr. Federico Rubio y Gali, 9
Madrid, 28039, Spain
Phone: 34-91-554-6484
Fax: 34-91-554-6487
Website: www.narceaediciones.es
Email: narcea@narceaediciones.es
Specialty Subjects: Humanities, Scientific and Technical Books, Sociology, Spiritual and Religious Books
Founded 1968 in Spain
Top Authors: Anselm Grün, Jerome Bruner, Miguel Angel Zabalza

Ediciones Norte, Inc.
PO Box 29461
San Juan, 00929-0461, Puerto Rico
Phone: 787-701-0909
Fax: 787-701-0922
Website: www.edicionesnorte.com
Email: info@edicionesnorte.com
Specialty Subjects: Children's Literature, Nutrition, Reference, Religion, Self-help, Textbooks
U.S. Sales: 10%
Founded 2001 in Puerto Rico
Top Authors: Agustín Sevillano, Chicola Mejia

Ediciones Nowtilus
Dona Juana I de Castilla, 44, 3-C
Madrid, 28027, Spain
Phone: 34-629-550-555
Fax: 34-914-377-958
Website: www.nowtilus.com
Email: santos@nowtilus.com
Specialty Subjects: Cookbooks, History and Anthropology, Science Fiction, Technology and Computer Science
U.S. Warehouse
U.S. Sales: 10%
Founded 2002 in Spain
Top Authors: Fernando Jiménez del Oso, Iñigo Pérez, Juan Antonio Cebrián

Ediciones Nuevo Espacio
53 Jackson St.
Fair Haven, NJ 07704
Fax: 732 933-1075
Website: www.editorial-ene.com

Email: ednuevoespacio@aol.com
Specialty Subjects: Academic Books, Fiction, Poetry
U.S. Warehouse
Distributors: Baker & Taylor
U.S. Sales: 95%
Founded 2000 in USA
Top Authors: Alejandro Gac-Artigas, Blanca Anderson, Carlos Guillermo Wilson

Ediciones Paidós Ibérica, S.A.
Mariano Cubi, 92
Barcelona, Spain
Phone: 34-93-241-9250
Fax: 34-93-202-2954
Website: www.paidos.com
Email: paidos@paidos.com
Specialty Subjects: Body and Health, Cinema, Communications, Oriental Studies, Parenting, Pedagogy, Philosophy, Self-help
Distributors: The Bilingual Publications Co., Books on Wings/Brodart Español, Chulainn, Lectorum
Founded 1979 in Spain
Top Authors: Erich Fromm, Nathaneil Branden, Stephen R. Covey

Ediciones Selectas Diamante, S.A. de C.V.
Convento de San Bernardo # 7
Col. Jardines de Santa Mónica
Tlalnepantla, 5400, México
Phone: 52-53-97-3132
Fax: 52-53-97-6020
Website: www.editorialdiamante.com
Email: ventas@editorialdiamante.com
Specialty Subjects: Self-help, Self-improvement
Distributors: Books on Wings/Brodart Español, Girón Books, International Enterprise, Lectorum, Libros Sin Fronteras, Magnamex, World Educational Inc.
U.S. Sales: 15%
Founded 1993 in México

Ediciones Serres, S.L.
Muntaner 391
Barcelona, 08021, Spain
Phone: 34-93-414-5746
Fax: 34-93-414-6581
Website: www.edicioneserres.com

Email: info@edicioneserres.com
Specialty Subjects: Children's Picture Books, Young Adult Books
Distributors: Lectorum
U.S. Sales: 16%
Founded in Spain
Top Authors: Jamie Lee Curtis, Lauren Child, Lucy Cousins

Ediciones Tecolote, S.A. de C.V.
Gobernador José Ceballos # 10
Col. San Miguel Chapultepec
México City, 11850, México
Phone: 52-55-5272-8085
Fax: 52-55-5272-8085
Website: www.edicionestecolote.com
Email: tecolote@edicionestecolote.com
Specialty Subjects: Art, Children and Young Adult, History
Distributors: Mariuccia Iaconi Books
Founded 1993 in México
Top Authors: José Joaquín Blanco, Krystyna Libura, Oscar Chávez

Ediciones Tutor, S.A.
Marques de Urquijo, 34
Madrid, 28008, Spain
Phone: 34-91-559-9832
Fax: 34-91-541-0235
Website: www.edicionestutor.com
Email: comercial@edicionestutor.com
Specialty Subjects: Crafts, Domestic Animals, Sports
Distributors: Lectorum, Libros Sin Fronteras, The Bilingual Publications Co.
U.S. Sales: 1%
Founded 1988 in Spain
Top Authors: Harvey Penick, John Updike, Monty Roberts

Ediciones Universal
3090 SW 8th St.
Miami, FL 33135
Phone: 305-642-3355
Fax: 305-642-7978
Website: www.ediciones.com
Email: ediciones@ediciones.com
Specialty Subjects: Books About Cuba, Literary Review
U.S. Warehouse

Distributors: Baker & Taylor, Ediciones Universal
U.S. Sales: 90%
Founded 1965 in USA
Top Authors: José Sánchez-Boudy, Lydia Cabrera, Reinaldo Arenas

Ediciones Verbo Vivo
Avda. Brasil 1864, Pueblo Libre
Lima, Peru
Phone: 511-475-3453
Email: adverbovivo@hotmail.com
U.S. Warehouse
Founded 1996 in Peru

Edilar, S.A. de C.V.
Blvd. Manuel Avila Camacho 1994,
Despacho 403
México City, México
Phone: 52-55-5361-96-11
Fax: 52-55-53-61-08-51
Website: www.clublectores.com
Email: club@clublectores.com
Imprints: Edilar
Founded 1994 in México
Top Authors: Eusebio Ruvalcaba, Vicente Leñero

Edimat Libros, S.A.
Primavera, 35
Polígono Industrial El Malvar
Madrid, 28500, Spain
Phone: 34-91-871-9088
Fax: 34-91-871-9071
Website: www.edimat.es
Email: edimat@edimat.es
Specialty Subjects: Cookbooks, Encyclopedias, History, Mythology, Self-help, Classics
Imprints: Edimat Libros, Estudio Didáctico
Distributors: IPG, Soundprints
U.S. Sales: 4%
Founded 1991 in Spain
Top Authors: Bernie Rowen, Miguel de Cervantes, Patricia Lamond

Editer's Publishing House
654 Schafer Place
Escondido, CA 92025
Phone: 619-339-7030

Fax: 760-294-2685
Website: www.editerspublishing.com
Email: contactus@editerspublishing.com
Specialty Subjects: Grammar and Spelling, Motivational, Novels, Poetry and Theater, World Literature
U.S. Warehouse
Distributors: Book Wholesalers, H.E. Learning Plans, Los Andes Publishing Company
U.S. Sales: 20%
Founded 1999 in USA
Top Authors: Emilio Rojas, José Joaquín Fernández De Lizardi, Luis Rodríguez Bandala

Editorial Acribia, S.A.
Royo, 23, Apartado Correos 466
Zaragoza, 50080, Spain
Phone: 34-97-623-2089
Fax: 34-97-621-9212
Website: www.editorialacribia.com
Email: acribia@red3.1.es
Specialty Subjects: Science
U.S. Sales: 5%
Founded 1957 in Spain
Top Authors: Belitz, Fennema

Editorial Albatros
Jerónimo Salguero 2745
5° Piso, Oficina 51
Buenos Aires, 1425, Argentina
Phone: 54-11-4807-2030
Fax: 54-11-4807-2010
Website: www.albatros.com.ar
Email: info@albatros.com.ar
Specialty Subjects: Children's Books, Cookbooks, Craft and Decorating, Gardening and Landscaping, Practical Homes
Distributors: Books on Wings/Brodart Español, Downtown Book Center, Mariuccia Iaconi Books, Lectorum
U.S. Sales: 2%
Founded 1950 in Argentina

Editorial Alfredo Ortells, S.L.
Sagunto, 5
Valencia, Spain
Phone: 34-96-347-1000
Fax: 34-96-347-3910

Website: www.ortells.com
Email: editorial@ortells.com
Specialty Subjects: Religion
Distributors: Mana Religious, Superior Imports
U.S. Sales: 10%
Founded 1952 in Spain
Top Authors: Estela Ortells, Esther González, Rvdo. Samuel Valero

Editorial Apóstrofe
c/Sierra de Albarracín, 3
Arganda del Rey, Spain
Phone: 34-90-219-5928
Fax: 34-90-219-5551
Website: www.edicionesapostrofe.com
Email: richard@stanleyformacion.com
Specialty Subjects: Art and Architecture, Historic Narrative, Management, Self-help
Imprints: Apóstrofe, Laberinto, Stanley
Distributors: Downtown Book Center, Libromundo
U.S. Sales: 2%
Founded in Spain
Top Authors: Federico Gan, Luisa Alba

Editorial Astrea de Alfredo y Ricardo Depalma SRL
Lavalle 1208
Buenos Aires, C4048AAF, Argentina
Phone: 54-11-4382-1880
Fax: 54-11-4382-1880
Website: www.astrea.com.ar
Email: info@astrea.com.ar
Specialty Subjects: Legal, Social Sciences
Founded 1968 in Argentina
Top Authors: Antonio Vázquez Vialard, Gustavo Bossert, Nestor Sagues

Editorial Avante, S.A. de C.V.
Luis González Obregón #9, Col. Centro
México City, México
Phone: 52-55-510-8804
Fax: 52-55-521-5245
Website: www.editorialavante.com.mx
Email: editorialavante@editorialavante.com.mx
Founded 1947 in México

Editorial Bonum
Av. Corrientes 6687
Buenos Aires, C1427BPE, Argentina
Phone: 54-11-4554-1414
Fax: 54-11-4554-1414
Website: www.editorialbonum.com.ar
Email: gerencia@editorialbonum.com.ar
Distributors: Downtown Book Center, Libros Sin Fronteras
U.S. Sales: 5%
Top Authors: Anselm Grün, Hermana Bernarda
Founded in Argentina

Editorial Casals, S.A.
c/Caspe 79
Barcelona, 08013, Spain
Phone: 34-93-244-9550
Fax: 34-93-265-6895
Website: www.editorialcasals.com
Email: casals@editorialcasals.com
Specialty Subjects: Biographies, Children's Videos, Religion, Textbooks
U.S. Sales: 5%
Founded 1870 in Spain
Top Authors: Fernando Lalana, María del Carmen de la Bandera, Susana Fernández Gabaldón

Editorial CEC, S.A. Los Libros de El Nacional
Maderero a Puente Nuevo
Galpón Así Es La Noticia, PB
Caracas, Venezuela
Phone: 58-212-408-3588
Fax: 58-212-408-3939
Website: www.libroselnacional.com
Email: libros@el-nacional.com
Specialty Subjects: Children and Young Adult, Cookbooks, General Interest, Literature, University Books
Distributors: The Bilingual Publications Co., Libros Sin Fronteras, Multicultural, Nana Books
Founded 1997 in Venezuela
Top Authors:
Arturo Uslar Pietri, J. D. Garcia Bacca

Editorial Celta Amaquemecan, A.C.
Bolivar Sierra, 29
Fraccionamiento Las Delicias
México City, México
Phone: 52-55-573-7900
Fax: 52-55-573-7900
Email: celtaamaquemecan@hotmail.com
Specialty Subjects: Children and Young
Adult Literature
Distributors: Aims International Books,
Bilingual Educational Services, Lectorum
Publications, Mariuccia Iaconi Book Imports,
The Bilingual Publications Co.
U.S. Sales: 60%
Founded 1982 in México
Top Authors: Gilberto Rendón Ortiz, Gilles
Tibo, Liliana Santirso, Martha Sastrías

Editorial Ciudad Argentina
c/Velázquez, 75, 2ndo izquierdo
Madrid, 28006, Spain
Phone: 34-91-577-0195
Fax: 34-91-575-6639
Website: www.ciudadargentina.com.ar
Email: ciudadargentina@infonegocio.com
Specialty Subjects: Business, History and
Social Sciences, Law
Distributors: Puvill
Founded 1983 in Argentina
Top Authors: Karol Woltyla, Roberto Dromi,
Roberto Lavagna

Editorial Colibrí, S.A. de C.V.
Sabino 63, Despacho 102
Col. Santa María La Ribera
México City, 06400, México
Phone: 52-55-47-14-66
Fax: 52-55-47-92-15
Website: www.edicolibri.com
Email: espartacorosales@edicolibri.com
Specialty Subjects: Essays, Narrative, Poetry
Founded 1999 in México
Top Authors: Alí Chumacero, Juan Bañuelos,
Vicente Quirarte

Editorial Conexión Gráfica, S.A. de C.V.
Libertad 1471,
Col. Americana
Guadalajara, 44100, México
Phone: 52-33-825-1565

Fax: 52-33-826-3104
Website: www.conexiongrafica.com.mx
Email:
conexiongrafica@conexiongrafica.com.mx
Specialty Subjects: Children's Books, Essays,
Novels
U.S. Sales: 1%
Founded 1985 in México
Top Authors: Magdalena González Casillas,
Marcia De Vere

Editorial Cordillera, Inc.
PO Box 192363
San Juan, 00919-2363, Puerto Rico
Phone: 787-767-6188
Fax: 787-767-8646
Website: www.editorialcordillera.com
Email: info@editorialcordillera.com
Specialty Subjects: Literature, Social Sciences
U.S. Sales: 5%
Founded 1966 in Puerto Rico
Top Authors: Luis Llorens Torres, Luis
López Nieves, Myriam Yagnam

Editorial Costa Rica
Guadalupe, Contiguo al Cementerio
San José, Costa Rica
Phone: 506-253-5354
Fax: 506-253-5091
Website: www.editorialcostarica.com
Email: difusion@editorialcostarica.com
Specialty Subjects: Children's and Young
Adult Literature, History, Literature from
Costa Rica, Novels, Poetry
U.S. Sales: 0%
Founded 1959 in Costa Rica
Top Authors: Ana Istarú, Jorge Debravo, Uriel
Quesada

Editorial del Valle de México, S.A. de C.V.
Constitución #35, Col. Escandón
México City, México
Phone: 52-55-5272-4556
Fax: 5255-5277-1513
Email: valledeMéxico@prodigy.net.mx
Specialty Subjects: General Interest, History
of México, Reference, Religion
U.S. Sales: 0%
Founded 1959 in México

Top Authors: Bernal Díaz del Castillo, Justo Sierra, Vicente Riva Palacio

Editorial Diana, S.A. de C.V.
Arenal #24, Edificio Norte, Col. Ex Hacienda Guadalupe Chimalistac
México City, 01050, México
Phone: 52-55-5089-1220
Fax: 52-55-5089-1248
Website: www.diana.com.mx
Email: ventas@diana.com.mx
Specialty Subjects: All Subjects
Distributors: The Bilingual Publications, Girón Books, Lectorum, Libros Sin Fronteras, Ritmo Latino
U.S. Sales: 18%
Founded 1946 in México
Top Authors: Elena Poniatowska, Gabriel García Márquez, Germán Dehesa

Editorial Gedisa Mexicana, S.A.
Guanajuato #202, Local 1, Col. Roma
México City, 06700, México
Phone: 52-55-5564-5607
Fax: 52-55-5564-7908
Website: www.gedisa.com
Email: jrcruz@mexis.com

Editorial Graó
Francesc Tàrrega, 32–34
Barcelona, Spain
Phone: 34-93-408-0464
Fax: 34-93-352-2437
Website: www.grao.com
Email: grao@grao.com
Specialty Subjects: Education
Founded 1977 in Spain
Top Authors: Antoni Zabala, Francesc Imbernón, Serafín Ant'nez

Editorial Guadal S.A./ El Gato de Hojalata
Pte. Julio A. Roca 546
Piso 3°, Oficina 1
Buenos Aires, Argentina
Phone: 54-11-4343-2055
Fax: 54-11-4343-2055
Website: www.editorialguadal.com.ar
Email: oarmayor@editorialguadal.com.ar
Specialty Subjects: Art, Children's Literature, History, Services

Founded 2002 in Argentina
Top Authors: O'Kif, Ricardo Mariño, Silvia Schujer

Editorial Guadalmena, S.L.
c/Vicente Aleixandre, 1
41500 Alcalá de Guadaíra
Sevilla, Spain
Phone: 34-95-410-0163
Fax: 34-95-410-0127
Email: editoguadalmena@hotmail.com
Specialty Subjects: Children's Books, Essays, Novels
Founded 1985 in Spain
Top Authors: Alberto Queraltó, José Nogales, Ruiz Lagos

Editorial Imaginador
Bartolomé Mitre 374
Buenos Aires, C1201AAS, Argentina
Phone: 54-11-4958-4111
Fax: 54-11-4958-4111
Website: www.imaginador.com.ar
Email: editorial@imaginador.com.ar
Specialty Subjects: Arts and Crafts, Cookbooks, Health and Spirituality, Hobbies, Mind and Boby, Supplemental Material
Distributors: The Bilingual Publications Co., Books on Wings/Brodart Español, Downtown Book Center, Lectorum, Libros Sin Fronteras, Spanish Language Book Services
U.S. Sales: 12%
Founded 1991 in Argentina
Top Authors: Alicia Pérez Cali, Elsa Felder, Luis Landriscina

Editorial INBio (Editorial del Instituto Nacional de Biodiversidad)
Del Cementerio de Santo Domingo
1 Bloque al Norte y Dos al Oeste
Heredia, Costa Rica
Phone: 506-507-8184
Fax: 506-507-8274
Website: www.inbio.ac.cr/editorial
Email: editorial@inbio.ac.cr
Specialty Subjects: Nature
U.S. Sales: 50%
Founded 2001 in Costa Rica

Top Authors: Dr. Barry Hammel, Dr. Garret Crow, Dr. Ginber Garrison

Editorial Juventud, S.A.
c/Provenza 101
Barcelona, 08029, Spain
Phone: 34-93-444-1800
Fax: 34-93-444-1802
Website: www.editorialjuventud.es
Email: info@editorialjuventud.es
Specialty Subjects: Children's Books, Classics, Biography, Nautilus Books.
U.S. Warehouse
Distributors: Adler's Books, The Bilingual Books Co., Lectorum
U.S. Sales: 25%
Founded 1929 in Spain
Top Authors: David Shannon, Jannell Cannon, Miguel de Cervantes

Editorial Kier, S.A.
Avda. Santa Fe 1260
Buenos Aires, Argentina
Phone: 54-11-4811-0507
Fax: 54-11-4811-3395
Website: www.kier.com.ar
Email: info@kier.com.ar
Specialty Subjects: Alternative Medicine, Self-help, Tarot, and Astrology
Founded 1907 in Argentina
Top Authors: Krishnamurti, Vivekananda, Darío Lostado

Editorial La Muralla, S.A.
Constancia, 33
Madrid, 28002, Spain
Phone: 34-91-416-1371
Fax: 34-91-413-5907
Website: www.arcomuralla.com
Email: muralla@arcomuralla.com
Specialty Subjects: Pedagogy, Statistics, Textbooks
U.S. Sales: 5%
Founded 1967 in Spain
Top Authors: Fernando Reimers, María Antonia Casanova, María Victoria Reyzábal

Editorial Limusa, S.A. de C.V.
Balderas 95
México City, 06040, México
Phone: 52-8503-8050
Fax: 52-5512-2903
Website: www.noriega.com.mx
Email: limusa@noriega.com.mx
Specialty Subjects: Art, School Textbooks, Technical books, University Textbooks
Imprints: Limusa, Limusa Wiley, Nori, Noriega Editores
U.S. Warehouse
Distributors: Spanish Language Book Services Inc.
U.S. Sales: 2%
Founded 1954 in México
Top Authors: Agustín Reyes Ponce, Gilberto Enríquez Harper, Janice Vancleave

Editorial Médica Panamericana
Alberto Alcocer, 24
Madrid, 28036, Spain
Phone: 34-91-131-7800
Fax: 34-91-457-0919
Website: www.medicapamericana.es
Email: info@medicapanamericana.es

Editorial Molino, S.L.
Calabria, 166
Barcelona, 08015, Spain
Phone: 34-93-226-0625
Fax: 34-93-226-698-98
Website: www.editorialmoli#es
Email: molino@menta.net
Specialty Subjects: Children and Young Adult Literature
Distributors: Aims International Books, Astran, Inc., Distribooks, Inc., Mariuccia Iaconi Book Import, La Moderna Poesía, Latin Trading Corporation, Lectorum, Libros Sin Fronteras, The Bilingual Publications Co.
U.S. Sales: 5%
Founded 1933 in Spain
Top Authors: Agatha Christie, Terry Deary, Tony Wolf

Editorial Océano de México, S.A. de C.V.
Eugenio Sue #59
Col. Chapultepec Polanco
Deleg. Miguel Hidalgo
México City, México
Phone: 52-55-5279-9000
Fax: 52-55-5279-9006

Website: www.oceano.com.mx
Email: export@oceano.com.mx
Specialty Subjects: Biographies, Children/
Young Adult, Dictionaries, Novels,
Photography/Art, Politics, Self-help, Classics
Imprints: Abraxas, Americo Arte, Circe,
Lengua de Trapo, Losada, Océano, Océano
Ambar, Océano CONACULTA, Océano
Turner, Salamandra, Turner
U.S. Warehouse
Distributors: All Major U.S. Distributors
U.S. Sales: 15%
Founded 1988 in México
Top Authors: Guadalupe Loaeza, Luis Spota,
Sara Sefchovich

Editorial Oveja Negra, Ltda.
Carrera 14, # 79–17
Bogotá, Colombia
Phone: 571-530-9678
Fax: 571-257-7900
Email: editovejanegra@latinmail.com
Specialty Subjects: Children and Young
Adult, Contemporary Literature, General
Interest, Politics, and Economics
U.S. Sales: 0%
Founded 1975 in Colombia
Top Authors: Gabriel García Márquez, Isabel
Allende, Marcela Serrano

Editorial Paidotribo
Consejo de Ciento, 245, bis 1ſ1™
Barcelona, 08011, Spain
Phone: 34-93-323-3311
Fax: 34-93-453-5033
Website: www.paidotribo.com
Email: paidotribo@paidotribo.com
Specialty Subjects: Arts and Crafts, Nutrition
and Health, Sports and Games
Imprints: Disfruto y Hago, Paidotribo
U.S. Sales: 3%
Founded 1986 in Spain
Top Authors: Busquet, Delavier, Wilmore

Editorial Pax México
Avda. Cuauhtemoc #1430
México City, 03310, México
Phone: 52-55-605-7677
Fax: 52-55-605-7600
Website: www.editorialpax.com

Email: editorialpax@editorialpax.com
Specialty Subjects: Psychology, Religions,
Self-help
Distributors: Books on Wings/Brodart
Español, Downtown Book Center, Girón,
Lectorum, Libros Sin Fronteras, Ritmo
Latino, Spanish Book Center, The Bilingual
Publications Co.
U.S. Sales: 20%
Founded 1960 in México
Top Authors: David Werner, Manuel
Lezaeta, Virginia Satir

Editorial Plaza Mayor, Inc.
1500 Ponce de León Ave.
Local 2–El Cinco
San Juan, 00926, Puerto Rico
Phone: 787-764-0455
Fax: 787-764-0465
Website: www.editorialplazamayor.com
Email: ventas@editorialplazamayor.com
Specialty Subjects: Cuban Literature, English
and Spanish Textbooks for Schools and
Universities, Puerto Rican Literature
U.S. Warehouse
Distributors: A & A Spanish Books, Bastos
Books, Ediciones Universal, Lectorum, Tres
Américas
U.S. Sales: 10%
Founded 1990 in Puerto Rico
Top Authors: Edgardo Rodríguez Juliá, José
Luis Vega, María Vaquero

Editorial Portavoz
PO Box 2607
Grand Rapids, MI 49501
Phone: 616-451-4775
Fax: 616-493-1790
Website: www.portavoz.com
Email: Portavoz@portavoz.com
Specialty Subjects: Religion
U.S. Warehouse
Distributors: Pan de Vida, Spring Arbor
U.S. Sales: 50%
Founded 1970 in USA
Top Authors: Elizabeth George, Erwin W.
Lutzer, John MacArthur

Editorial Saure, S.A.
P.I. Goiain, Avda. San Blas, 11
01170 Legutiano
Alava, Spain
Phone: 34-94-546-5825
Fax: 34-94-546-5825
Website: www.ed-saure.com
Email: saure@ed-saure.com
Specialty Subjects: Comic Books
Distributors: Barataria
Founded 2002 in Spain
Top Authors: Daniel Redondo, Nathalie
Bodin, Pello Gutiérrez

Editorial Sigmar, S.A.
Avda. Belgrano 1580
Buenos Aires, 1093, Argentina
Phone: 54-11-4381-1715
Fax: 54-11-4383-5633
Website: www.sigmar.com.ar
Email: export@sigmar.com.ar
Specialty Subjects: Children's and Young
Adult Books
Distributors: The Bilingual Publications Co.,
Mariuccia Iaconi Books, Lectorum, Libros
Sin Fronteras, Los Andes
Founded 1941 in Argentina
Top Authors: Graciela Montes, Ricardo
Marino, Susana Martín

Editorial Sin Límites
9737 NW 41 St., Suite 413
Miami, FL 33178
Phone: 305-716-9749
Fax: 305-592-3362
Website: www.sinlimites.net
Email: info@sinlimites.net
Specialty Subjects: Spiritual and Metaphysics
Imprints: 14 Spanish-language imprints.
U.S. Warehouse
Distributors: Editorial Sin Límites
U.S. Sales: 35%
Founded 1992 in USA
Top Authors: Ferguson, Ramtha, Whitworth

Editorial Sirpus S.L.
Cardenal Vives i Tutó, 59, bajos
Barcelona, Spain
Phone: 34-93-206-3772
Fax: 34-93-280-1234

Website: www.sirpus.com
Email: info@sirpus.com
Specialty Subjects: Business, Narrative and
Essays, Poetry, Psychology, Spiritual, Travel
Distributors: The Bilingual Publications Co.,
Mariuccia Iaconi Books, Lectorum
U.S. Sales: 3%
Founded 1996 in Spain
Top Authors: Carlos Cañeque, Elisabeth
Kübler-Ross

Editorial Stanley
c/Mendelu, 15
Honbarridia, Spain
Phone: 34-94-364-0412
Fax: 34-94-364-3863
Website: www.stanleyformacion.com
Email: richard@stanleyformacion.com
Specialty Subjects: Foreign Language Books
Imprints: ELI, Express Publishing, Stanley
Distributors: Downtown Book Center,
Libromundo
U.S. Sales: 1%
Founded 1991 in Spain
Top Authors: Edward R. Rosset, Glenn
Darragh

**Editorial Sudamericana–Random House
Mondadori Argentina**
Humberto Primo 555
Buenos Aires, C1103 ACK, Argentina
Phone: 54-11-5235-4427
Fax: 54-11-5235-4468
Website: www.edsudamericana.com.ar
Email: comexterior@edsudamericana.com.ar
Specialty Subjects: All subject areas
U.S. Warehouse
U.S. Sales: 1%
Founded 1939 in Argentina
Top Authors: Dale Carnegie, Gabriel García
Márquez, Jorge Bucay

Editorial Trillas
Av. Rio Churubusco 385, Pte
Col. Pedro María Anaya
México City, 03340, México
Phone: 52-55-5633-1112
Fax: 52-55-5634-2221
Website: www.trillas.com.mx
Email: laviga@trillas.com.mx

Editorial Unilit
1360 NW 88 Ave.
Miami, FL 33172
Phone: 305-592-6136
Fax: 305-592-0087
Website: www.editorialunilit.com
Specialty Subjects: Children, Inspirational, Religion
Imprints: Editorial Unilit
U.S. Warehouse
Distributors: All Major Distributors
U.S. Sales: 57%
Founded 1974 in USA
Top Authors: Gary Chapman, James Dobson, Stormie Omartian

Editorial Vicens Vives
Avda. Sarria 130-132
Barcelona, 08017, Spain
Phone: 34-93-252-3705
Fax: 34-93-252-3712
Website: www.vicenvives.es
Email: export@vicenvives.es
Specialty Subjects: Literature, Elementary and College Textbooks
Distributors: ABC Book Supply, Gama, Lectorum, Libros Sin Fronteras, Los Andes Publishing, Mariuccia Iaconi Books
Founded 1961 in Spain
Top Authors: Antonio Fernández, Javier Fraile

Editorial y Distribuidora Leo, S.A. de C.V.
Calle Melesio Morales 16
Col. Guadalupe Inn.
México City, 01020, México
Phone: 52-55-6641454
Fax: 52-55-6605561
Website: www.editorialscorpio.com.mx
Email: edilibra@prodigy.net.mx
Imprints: Géminis, Leo, Libra
Distributors: Amazon, Lectorum
U.S. Sales: 7%
Founded 1992 in México
Top Authors: Dina Von Braune, Dr. Marisela Camacho

Editorial Zendrera Zariquiey, S.A.
Cardenal Vives i Tuto, 59 Bajos
Barcelona, 08034, Spain
Phone: 34-93-280-1234

Fax: 34-93-280-6190
Website: www.editorialzendrera.com
Email: info@editorialzendrera.com
Specialty Subjects: Gastronomy
Distributors: The Bilingual Publications Co., Lectorum, Mariuccia Iaconi Books
U.S. Sales: 8%
Founded 1997 in Spain
Top Authors: Claudia Roden, Jane Hissey, Patricia Wells

Educational Services Corporation
P.O. Box 797
Rockville, MD 20848-0797
Phone: 301-374-9008
Fax: 301-374-2216
U.S. Warehouse
Distributors: Ingram
U.S. Sales: 90%
Founded 1948 in USA

Edufam Ediciones S.A. de C.V.
Maximino A. Camacho 63–1
Col. Nápoles, Deleg., Benito Juárez, C.P.
México City, 03810, México
Phone: 52-55-563-1558
Fax: 52-55-5611-8978
Email: edufammx@yahoo.com
Specialty Subjects: Religion, Self-improvement, Technology
Founded 2001 in México
Top Authors: Carlos Alvear García García, Ma. Icaza, Manuel Jiménez

Espacio Editorial
Bolívar 547, 3° Piso. Of. 1
Bueno Aires, Argentina
Phone: 54-11-4331-1945
Fax: 54-11-4331-1945
Website: www.espacioeditorial.com.ar
Email: espacioedit@ciudad.com.ar
Specialty Subjects: Ecology and Environment, Education, Social Sciences, Social Work
U.S. Sales: 1%
Founded 1992 in Argentina
Top Authors: Carlos Eroles, Estela Gras, Margarita Rosas

Esperanza Group, Inc.
3810 W. 26th St., 2nd Floor
Chicago, IL 60623
Phone: 773-521-3100
Fax: 773-762-8845
Website: www.esperanzagroup.com
Email: j.Gomez@esperanzagroup.com
Specialty Subjects: Self-help
U.S. Warehouse
Distributors: Baker & Taylor, Distribooks
U.S. Sales: 100%
Founded 1999 in USA
Top Authors: Rosalba Pioa

Evan-Moor Educational Publishers
18 Lower Ragsdale
Monterey, CA 93940
Phone: 831-649-5901
Fax: 831-649-6256
Website: www.evan-moor.com
Email: sales@evan-moor.com
Specialty Subjects: Supplemental
Educational Material for Grades PreK–6
U.S. Warehouse
Distributors: Book Clubs, Bookstores, Trade
Shows
U.S. Sales: 94%
Founded 1979 in USA

F&G Editores/F&G Libros de Guatemala
31 Ave. "C" 5–54 Zona 7
Col. Centroamérica
Guatemala City, Guatemala
Phone: 502-433-2361
Fax: 502-433-2361
Website: www.fygeditores.com
Email: fgeditor@guate.net.gt
Specialty Subjects: Guatemalan Literature,
Social Sciences
Distributors: Books On Wings/Brodart
Español, Libros Sin Fronteras, The Bilingual
Publications Co., Vientos Tropicales
U.S. Sales: 2%
Founded 1994 in Guatemala
Top Authors: Eugenia Gallardo, Marco
Antonio Flores

FC Editorial
c/Arivro Sorio, 311
Madrid, 28083, Spain

Phone: 34-91-384-6530
Fax: 34-91-384-6531
Website: www.fundacionconfemetal.com
Email: editorial@fundacionconfemetal.com

Feierabend Verlag
c/o International Book Marketing
PO Box 8439
Princeton, NJ 08534
Phone: 609-936-1551
Fax: 609-936-1599
Website: www.feierabendverlag.de
Email: anne.marquess@verizon.net
Specialty Subjects: Photography and Art
U.S. Warehouse
Distributors: CDS, Jackson, TN
Founded 2001 in Germany

Firefly Books Ltd.
66 Leek Crescent
Richmond Hill, ON
L4B 1H1, Canada
Phone: 416-499-8412
Fax: 416-499-8313
Website: www.fireflybooks.com
Email: service@fireflybooks.com
Specialty Subjects: Spanish Children's Books
U.S. Sales: 1%
Founded 1974 in Canada
Top Authors: Dan Liebman, Debbie Bailey,
Robert Munsch

Floricanto Press
650 Castro, Suite 120331
Mountain View, CA 94041-2055
Phone: 415-552-1879
Fax: 702-995-1410
Website: www.floricantopress.com
Email: info@floricantopress.com
Specialty Subjects: Latin American Fiction,
Mexican American, Nonfiction, U.S.
Hispanics
Imprints: Floricanto Press
U.S. Warehouse
Distributors: Amazon.com, B&N, Blackwell
NA, Book House, Ingram, Midwest Library
Services, Yankee Book Peddler
U.S. Sales: 60%
Founded 1983 in USA

Top Authors: Bonny Hayman, Burton Moore, Carlos Mock

Fondo de Cultura Económica USA, Inc.
2293 Vreus St.
San Diego, CA 92154
Phone: 619-429-0455
Fax: 619-429-0827
Website: www.fceusa.com
Email: sales@fceusa.com
Specialty Subjects: Anthropology, Art, Children's Literature, History, Literary Reviews, Mexican and Latin American Literature, Politics and Economics, Science
U.S. Warehouse
Distributors: Adler's Foreign Books, Atanasio & Associates, Baker & Taylor, Brodart, Mariuccia Iaconi Book Imports, Ideal Foreign Books, Ingram, Lectorum, Libros Sin Fronteras
U.S. Sales: 5%
Founded 1934 in México
Top Authors: Juan Rulfo, Octavio Paz, Rosario Castellanos

Foreign Affairs in Spanish
Río Hondo # 1
Col. Tizapán San Angel
México City 01000, México
Phone: 52-55-628-4000
Fax: 52-55-628-4092
Website: www.foreignaffairs-esp.org
Email: dforaesp@itam.mx
Specialty Subjects: International Relations, Latin American Politics
Distributors: Word Wide Media
U.S. Sales: 6%
Founded 2000 in México
Top Authors: Carlos Salinas de Gortari, José Woldenberg, Vicente Fox

Forsa Editores
1594 Piñero Ave., Caparra Terrace
San Juan, PR 00921-1413
Phone: 888-225-8984
Fax: 787-707-1797
Website: www.forsaeditores.com
Email: info@forsaeditores.com
Specialty Subjects: Fiction
U.S. Warehouse

U.S. Sales: 25%
Founded 1994 in Puerto Rico
Top Authors: Luis Dávila Colón

Fundación Santa María Ediciones SM
Impresores, 15, Urb. Prado del Espino
Boadilla del Monte
Madrid, 28660, Spain
Phone: 34-91-422-8800
Fax: 34-91-422-6109
Website: www.grupo-sm.com
Email: international@grupo-sm.com
Specialty Subjects: Children's and Young Adult Literature
Distributors: ABC's Book Supply, The Bilingual Publications Co., Books On Wings/Brodart Español, Continental Book, Donars Spanish Books, Lectorum, Libros Sin Fronteras, Mariuccia Iaconi Books
U.S. Sales: 8%
Founded 1948 in Spain
Top Authors: Georgia Byng, Hilda Perera, Laura Gallego

Gallopade International
PO Box 2779
Peachtree City, GA 30269
Phone: 800-536-2438
Fax: 800-871-2979
Website: www.gallopade.com
Email: orders@gallopade.com
Specialty Subjects: Educational Supplemental Material for Children
Imprints: Black Jazz, Fiesta! Siesta! And all the Resta!, Pizzazz and Razzmatazz, The Carole Marsh Mysteries
U.S. Warehouse
Distributors: Baker & Taylor, Ingram, Newsgroup, Partners
U.S. Sales: 100%
Founded 1979 in USA

Gareth Stevens, Inc.
330 West Olive St., Suite 100
Milwaukee, WI 53212
Phone: 414-322-3520
Fax: 414-332-3567
Website: www.garethstevens.com
Email: info@gspub.com

Specialty Subjects: Arts and Crafts, Biographies, Early Literacy, Nature, Children's Nonfiction and Fiction, Science, Social Studies
Imprints: Gareth Stevens Publishing, Weekly Reader™ Early Learning Library, World Almanac™ Library
U.S. Warehouse
Founded 1983 in USA

Gingerbread House
602 Montauk Hwy.
Westhampton Beach, NY 11978
Phone: 631-288-5119
Fax: 631-288-5179
Website: www.Gingerbreadbooks.com
Email: GHBooks@optonline.net
U.S. Warehouse
U.S. Sales: 90%
Founded 1999 in USA
Top Authors: Dasha Ziborova, Josephine Nobisso

Girón Books, Inc.
2130 W. 21st St.
Chicago, IL 60608
Phone: 773-847-3000
Fax: 773-847-9197
Website: www.gironbooks.com
Email: sales@gironbooks.com
Specialty Subjects: Natural Health
Imprints: Girón Publishing
U.S. Warehouse
Distributors: Girón Books
U.S. Sales: 12%
Founded 2003 in USA
Top Authors: César Armoza

Global Software Publishing
535 West 34th St.
New York, NY 10001
Phone: 646-792-2793
Fax: 646-792-2112
Website: www.LearnAtGlobal.com
Email: Ilise@gspna.com
Specialty Subjects: Children's Software Publishing
Imprints: Dorling Kindersley
U.S. Warehouse

U.S. Sales: 100%
Founded 2001 in USA

Globus Publishing, LLC
5424 NW 94th, Doral Place
Miami, FL 33178
Phone: 305-718-8340
Fax: 305-718-8342
Email: nestorz@att.net
Specialty Subjects: Literature
U.S. Warehouse
U.S. Sales: 90%
Founded 2003 in USA
Top Authors: Eduardo García Aguilar, Jesús Zarate, Minelys Sánchez

Grolier Online (Scholastic Library Publishing)
90 Old Sherman Turnpike
Danbury, CT 06816
Phone: 888-326-6546 option 4
Website: go.grolier.com
Email: gosupport@scholasticlibrary.com
Imprints: Children's Press, Franklin Watts, Grolier, Grolier Online
U.S. Warehouse
Founded in USA

Granta en Español
Diagonal 662
Barcelona, 08034, Spain
Phone: 34-93-492-8823
Fax: 34-93-496-7051
Email: vmiles@planeta.es
Specialty Subjects: Current Events, Narrative, Short Fiction
U.S. Warehouse
Distributors: Planeta Publishing
Founded in Spain
Top Authors: Guillermo Cabrera Infante, Javier Marías, Susan Sontag

Grito Sagrado Editorial
11 de Setiembre 992, Piso 7
Buenos Aires, Argentina
Phone: 54-11-4775-9228
Fax: 54-11-4777-6765
Website: www.gritosagrado.com
Email: rpg@gritosagrado.com.ar

Groundwood Books/Libros Tigrillo
720 Bathurst St., Suite 500
Toronto, ON M5S 2R4, Canada
Phone: 416-537-2501
Fax: 416-537-4647
Website: www.groundwoodbooks.com
Email: genmail@groundwood-dm.com
Specialty Subjects: Children's Books
U.S. Warehouse
Distributors: Publishers Group West
Founded 1978 in Canada
Top Authors: Brian Doyle, Deborah Ellis,
Marie-Louise Gay

Grupo Anaya
c/Juan Ignacio Luca de Tena, 15
Madrid, 28027, Spain
Phone: 34-91-393-8700
Fax: 34-91-742-4259
Website: www.anaya.es
Email: cga.exportacion@anaya.es

Grupo Editorial 33, S.L.
Avda. Manuel Agustín Heredia, 12, 1f
Málaga, 29001, Spain
Phone: 34-60-781-4375
Fax: 34-95-260-8990
Email: grupo33@metrored-online.com
Specialty Subjects: Children's Books, History,
Medicine, Narrative
U.S. Sales: 0%
Founded 2001 in Spain
Top Authors: Esteban Alcántara, José María
Porta

Grupo Editorial Bruño, S.L.
Maestro Alonso 21
Madrid, 28028, Spain
Phone: 34-91-724-4897
Fax: 34-91-725-8359
Website: www.editorial-bruno.es
Email: eroussel@editorial-bruno.es
Specialty Subjects: Children's Literature,
Reference Books, Supplemental Material.
Distributors: Lectorum, Libros Sin
Fronteras.
U.S. Sales: 1%
Founded 1889 in Spain
Top Authors: Concha López Narváez, Jordi
Sierra i Fabra, Montserrat del Amo.

Grupo Editorial Lumen
Viamonte 1674
Buenos Aires, C1055ABF, Argentina
Phone: 54-11-4373-1414
Fax: 51-11-4375-0453
Website: www.lumen.com.ar
Email: editorial@lumen.com.ar
Specialty Subjects: Children's and Young
Adult, Psychology, Religion, Self-help,
Spiritual
Distributors: SEPI Books
Founded 1958 in Argentina
Top Authors: Anselm Grün, Anthony de
Mello, Henri Nouwen

Grupo Hispano Editorial
Aztecas 33, Col. Santa Cruz Acatlán
Naucalpan, 53150, México
Phone: 52-55-5360-3139
Fax: 52-55-5360-5851
Website: www.pgw.com
Email: sandras@pgw.com
Specialty Subjects: Architecture, Art,
Cookbooks, Design and Decor, Young Adult.
Imprints: Numen & Desgustis, Silver
Dolphin en Español
U.S. Warehouse
Distributors: Publishers Group West
Founded 2000 in México

Gryphon House, Inc.
1076 Tucker St.
Beltsville, MD 20704
Phone: 301-595-9500
Fax: 301-595-0051
Website: www.ghbooks.com
Email: info@ghbooks.com
Specialty Subjects: Early Childhood
Education
Imprints: Robins Lane Press
U.S. Warehouse
Distributors: Consortium Books &
Distribution
Founded 1971 in USA
Top Authors: Diane Trister Dodge, Katie
Kissinger, MaryAnn Kohl, Pam Schiller

Guilford Publications
72 Spring St.
New York, NY 10012
Phone: 212-431-9800
Fax: 212-966-6708
Website: www.guilford.com
Email: info@guilford.com
Specialty Subjects: Trade and Professional
Books in Psychology, Psychiatry, Behavioral
Sciences, Education, Geography and
Communications
Imprints: Guilford Press
U.S. Warehouse
Distributors: Academic Book Center, Baker
& Taylor, Blackwell's Book Services, Book
House, Brodart, Coutts Library Services,
Eastern Book Co., Ingram, JA Majors,
Matthews Book Co., MBS Book Exchange,
Mid-West Library Service, NACSCORP,
Rittenhouse, Yankee Book Peddler
Founded 1973 in USA
Top Authors: Christine Padesky, Jose
Bauermeister, Russell Barkley

**Harcourt Trade Publishers, Children's
Books Division**
252 B St., Suite 1900
San Diego, CA 92101
Phone: 619-231-6616
Fax: 619-699-6851
Website: www.HarcourtBooks.com
Specialty Subjects: Children's Books, Fiction,
Nonfiction
Imprints: Gulliver Books/Harcourt, Harcourt
Children's Books, Harcourt Young Classics,
Magic Carpet Books, Odyssey Classics, Red
Wagon Books/Harcourt, Silver Whistle/
Harcourt, Voyager Books
U.S. Warehouse
Founded 1919 in USA

Harlequin Enterprises, Ltd.
225 Duncan Mill Rd.
Don Mills, ON M3B 3K9, Canada
Phone: 416-445-5860
Fax: 416-448-7144
Website: www.eharlequin.com
Specialty Subjects: Women's Fiction with
Focus on Romance

Imprints: Harlequin, HQN, Luna, Mira, Red
Dress Ink, Steeple Hill
U.S. Warehouse
Distributors: Anderson, Barnes and Noble,
Borders, Kmart, Walden, Walmart
Founded 1949 in Canada

HarperCollins Publishers–Rayo
10 E 53rd St.
New York, NY 10022
Phone: 212-207-7787
Fax: 212-207-6978
Website: www.HarperCollins.com
Email: JeanMarie.Kelly@HarperCollins.com
Specialty Subjects: Children's Nonfiction and
Fiction, General Fiction and Nonfiction
Imprints: Rayo
U.S. Warehouse
Founded 2001 in USA
Top Authors: Isabel Allende, Jorge Ramos,
Paulo Coelho

Harvest Sun Press
PO Box 826
Fairacres, NM 88033
Phone: 479-283-4000
Fax: 505-526-6930
Website: www.harvestsunpress.com
Email: info@harvestsunpress.com
Specialty Subjects: Bilingual Children's
Books
Distributors: Amazon.com, Baker & Taylor,
Biblio, Book Wholesalers, Inc., Brodart
U.S. Sales: 100%
Founded 2003 in USA
Top Authors: Irving Torres, Lorenzo Liberto

HCI Español
3201 SW 15 St.
Deerfield Beach, FL 33442
Phone: 800-851-9100
Fax: 800-424-7652
Website: www.hcibooks.com
Email: editorial@hcibooks.com
Specialty Subjects: Inspirational, Self-help
U.S. Warehouse
U.S. Sales: 90%
Founded 2003 in USA

Hippocrene Books
171 Madison Ave., Suite 1602
New York, NY 10016
Phone: 212-685-4371
Fax: 212-779-9338
Website: www.hippocrenebooks.com
Email: Hippocrene.books@verizon.net
Specialty Subjects: Bilingual Reference,
Literature
U.S. Warehouse
U.S. Sales: 85%
Founded 1974 in USA
Top Authors: Enriqueta Rodriguez
Carrington, Ila Warner, Jose Serrano

Hunter House Publishers
1515 1/2 Park St.
Alameda, CA 94501
Phone: 510-865-5282
Fax: 510-865-4295
Website: www.hunterhouse.com
Email: hhi@hunterhouse.com
Specialty Subjects: Chronic Illness, Family
and Relationships, Parenting, Sexuality,
Health and Fitness, Self-help
Imprints: SmartFun Books
U.S. Warehouse
Distributors: Publishers Group West
Founded 1976 in USA
Top Authors: Barbara Keesling Ph.D., Linda
Ojeda Ph.D., Shawn Talbott Ph.D.

Iberoamericana Editorial Vervuert, S.L.
c/Amor de Dios, 1
Madrid, 28014, Spain
Phone: 34-91-429-3522
Fax: 34-91-429-5397
Website: www.ibero-americana.net
Email: info@iberoamericanalibros.com
Specialty Subjects: Essays, History,
Linguistics, Literary Reviews
U.S. Warehouse
Distributors: Latin American Book Source
U.S. Sales: 30%
Founded 1977 in Spain
Top Authors: Ignacio Arellano, John
Beverley, Mabel Moraña

Ideals Publications
535 Metroplex Dr., Suite 250

Nashville, TN 37211
Phone: 800-586-2572
Fax: 615-781-1447
Website: www.idealsbooks.com
Email: dtimson@guideposts.org
Specialty Subjects: Children's Board Books
and Picture Books, Gift Books
Imprints: Candy Cane Press, Guideposts,
Ideals, Ideals Children's Books, Ideals Press,
Williamson Books
U.S. Warehouse
Distributors: Baker & Taylor, Ingram, Koen,
Lectorum
U.S. Sales: 95%
Founded 1945 in USA
Top Authors: P.K Hallinan, Patricia A.
Pingry, Patricia Eubanks

Inner Traditions–Bear and Company
One Park St.
Rochester, VT 05767
Phone: 800-246-8648
Fax: 802-767-3726
Website: www.InnerTraditions.com
Email: orders@InnerTraditions.com
Specialty Subjects: Ancient Cultures, Art,
Health, New Age, Self-help, Spirituality
Imprints: Inner Traditions in Spanish
U.S. Warehouse
Distributors: All Major Distributors
U.S. Sales: 2%
Founded 1977 in USA
Top Authors: Alex Grey, Colleen Craig,
Harrish Johari

Instituto de Estudios Económicos
Castello, 128, 6 Planta
Madrid, 28006, Spain
Phone: 34-91-782-0580
Fax: 34-91-562-3613
Website: www.ieemadrid.com
Email: iee@ieemadrid.com

**Instituto Tecnológico y de Estudios
Superiores de Occidente**
Periférico Sur Manuel Gómez Morín 8585,
Tlaquepaque, Jalisco, México
Phone: 52-33-3669-3485
Fax: 52-33-3669-3485
Website: www.publicaciones@iteso.mx

Email: gabyva@iteso.mx
Specialty Subjects: Architecture and Design, Law and Politics, Literature, Social Sciences, Sociology
U.S. Sales: 10%
Founded 1990 in México
Top Authors: Michel de Certeau, Niklas Luhmann, Rossana Reguillo Cruz

Intercultural Center for Research in Education
366 Massachusetts Ave.
Arlington, MA 02474
Phone: 781-643-2142
Fax: 781-643-1315
Website: www.incre.org
Email: jzuman@incre.org
Specialty Subjects: Early Childhood Education, Educational Publishing, Multicultural Children's Books, Multicultural Science and Environmental Books
U.S. Sales: 94%
Founded 1990 in USA
Top Authors: Dr. Nancy Barra

Judson Press
PO Box 851
Valley Forge, PA 19482
Phone: 610-768-2135
Fax: 610-768-2107
Website: www.judsonpress.com
Email: info@judsonpress.com
Specialty Subjects: Bible Study, Pastor's Resources and Women's Issues, Sermon Resources
Imprints: Judson Press
U.S. Warehouse
Distributors: Anchor, Appalachian Inc., Baker & Taylor, Spring Arbor
U.S. Sales: 99%
Founded 1824 in USA
Top Authors: Bill J. Leonard, Lora-Ellen McKinney, Marvin A. McMickle

Kalandraka Editora
Alemania 70
Pontevedra, 36162, Spain
Phone: 34-98-686-0276
Fax: 34-98-610-0280
Website: www.kalandraka.com

Email: editora@kalandraka.com
Specialty Subjects: Children's Literature
Distributors: The Bilingual Publications Co., Books on Wings/Brodart Español, Lectorum, Libros Sin Fronteras, Mibi Books
U.S. Sales: 8%
Founded 1998 in Spain
Top Authors: Arnold Lobel, Mercer Meyer, Michael Grejniec

Language Success Press
2232 S. Main St., #345
Ann Arbor, MI 48103
Phone: 734-994-8578
Fax: 303-484-2004
Website: www.languagesuccesspress.com
Email: info@languagesuccesspress.com
Specialty Subjects: ESL
U.S. Warehouse
Distributors: Baker & Taylor, Bookazine
U.S. Sales: 90%
Founded 2003 in USA
Top Authors: Amy Gillett

Lectorum Publications, Inc.
205 Chubb Ave.
Lyndhurst, NJ 07071
Phone: 800-345-5946
Fax: 877-532-8676
Website: www.lectorum.com
Specialty Subjects: Children's and Young Adult Fiction and Nonfiction
U.S. Warehouse
U.S. Sales: 99%
Founded 1961 in USA
Top Authors: Marc Brown

Lee & Low Books, Inc.
95 Madison Ave., Suite 606
New Year, NY 10016
Phone: 212-779-4400 ext. 27
Fax: 212-683-1894
Website: www.leeandlow.com
Email: jlow@leeandlow.com
Specialty Subjects: Children's Fiction and Nonfiction
Imprints: Bebop Books
U.S. Warehouse
Distributors: Self-distributed
U.S. Sales: 95%

Founded 1991 in USA
Top Authors: Cheif Jake Swamp, Ken
Mochizuiki, William Miller

Lexicon Training Services
640 S. San Vicente Blvd
Los Angeles, CA 90048
Phone: 800-411-6666
Fax: 323-782-7347
Website: www.lexiconmarketing.com
Email: institutions@lexiconmarketing.com
Specialty Subjects: ESL
U.S. Warehouse
Distributors: Delta Catalogs and NES, Texas
Founded 1989 in USA

Liturgical Press
St John's Abbey
Collegeville, MN 656321
Phone: 800-858-5450
Fax: 800-445-5899
Website: www.litpress.org
Email: sales@litpress.org
Specialty Subjects: Liturgy, Monasticism,
Spirituality, Theology
Imprints: Michael Glazier, Pueblo Books
U.S. Warehouse
Distributors: Baker & Taylor, Ingram
U.S. Sales: 85%
Founded 1926 in USA

Liturgy Training Publications
1800 N. Hermitage Ave.
Chicago, IL 60622
Phone: 800-933-1800
Fax: 800-933-7094
Website: www.ltp.org
Email: orders@ltp.org
Specialty Subjects: Religion
Imprints: Catechesis of the Good Shepherd,
Hillenbrand Books
U.S. Warehouse
Distributors: Baker & Taylor, Ingram
U.S. Sales: 90%
Founded 1964 in USA
Top Authors: Carlos Maciel, Paul Turner,
Sofia Cavalletti

Lom Ediciones
Concha y Toro, 23
Santiago, Chile
Phone: 562-688-5273
Fax: 562-696-6388
Website: www.lom.cl
Email: lom@lom.cl
Specialty Subjects: Literature, Social Sciences
Distributors: The Latin American Book
Store
U.S. Sales: 2%
Founded 1990 in Chile
Top Authors: Elicura Chihuailaf, Ramón
Díaz Eterovic, Tomás Moulian

Longseller, S.A.
Avda. San Juan 777
Buenos Aires, Argentina
Phone: 54-11-5031-5400
Fax: 54-11-5031-5453
Website: www.longseller.com.ar
Email: comercioexterior@longseller.com.ar
Specialty Subjects: Biographies, Children
and Young Adult, Literature, Parenting, Self-
help, Spiritual, Values and Quality of Life
Imprints: Deva's, Era Naciente, Errepar,
Libris, Longseller, Sai Ram
Distributors: Advanced Marketing,
Downtown Book Center, Lectorum, Perrone,
Publishers Group West, Spanish Periodicals
U.S. Sales: 3%
Founded 2000 in Argentina
Top Authors: Anton Ponce De León, Eileen
Caddy, Nerio Tello

Mariuccia Iaconi Book Imports, Inc.
970 Tennessee St.
San Francisco, CA 94107
Phone: 800-955-9577
Fax: 415-821-1596
Website: www.iaconibooks.com
Email: mibibook@earthlink.net
Specialty Subjects: Children's Books
Imprints: Mariuccia Iaconi SF
U.S. Warehouse
Distributors: Mariuccia Iaconi
U.S. Sales: 100%
Founded 1995 in USA
Top Authors: Gianni Rodari, Janette Winters

Marsay Ediciones
Polígono Servialsa C/B # 34
Sevilla, 41960, Spain
Phone: 34-95-471-6618
Fax: 34-95-471-6618
Website: www.marsayediciones.com
Email: marsay@marsayediciones.com
Specialty Subjects: Religion, Self-help
Founded in Spain
Top Authors: Joseph de Maistre, Martínez de
Pasqually

Mason Crest Publishers
370 Reed Rd., Suite 302
Broomall, PA 19008
Phone: 610-543-6200
Fax: 610-543-3878
Website: www.masoncrest.com
Email: cschultz@masoncrest.com
Specialty Subjects: Biography, Geography,
Health, History
U.S. Warehouse
Distributors: Barker & Taylor, Brodart,
Follett, Ingram
Founded 2001 in USA
Top Authors: Mayo Clinic

Mosaic Press
1252 Speers Rd, Units 1 & 2
Oakville, ON, L6L 5N9, Canada
Phone: 800-387-8992
Fax: 800-387-8992
Website: www.mosaic-press.com
Email: mosaicpress@on.aibn.com
Specialty Subjects: Cultural Studies, Fiction,
International Studies, Multicultural
Literature, Poetry, Social Studies, Spanish-
language and Bilingual Spanish Books,
Theatre
U.S. Warehouse
Distributors: SCB
U.S. Sales: 50%
Founded 1976 in Canada
Top Authors: Irving Layton, Joy Kogawa,
Pablo Armando Fernández

Mundi-Prensa Libros, S.A.
c/Castello, 37
Madrid, 28001, Spain
Phone: 34-91-436-3704

Fax: 34-91-575-3998
Websites: www.mundiprensa.com and
www.mundilibro.com
Email: libreria@mundiprensa.es
Specialty Subjects: Agriculture and
Environment, Natural Sciences
Distributors: Distributed from our office in
México
Founded 1948 in Spain
Top Authors: Ginés López, José Antonio del
Cañizo, José Vicente Maroto

New World Library
14 Pamaron Way
Novato, CA 94949
Phone: 415-884-2100
Fax: 415-884-2199
Website: www.newworldlibrary.com
Email: escort@newworldlibrary.com
Specialty Subjects: Personal Growth,
Spirituality
U.S. Warehouse
Distributors: Baker & Taylor, Ingram, New
Leaf, Publishers Group West
Founded 1977 in USA
Top Authors: Deepak Chopra

Noguer y Caralt Editores, S.A.
Santa Amelia, 22
Barcelona, 08024, Spain
Phone: 34-93-280-1399
Fax: 34-93-280-1993
Website: www.noguercaralt.com
Email: contact@noguercaralt.com

Norma Editorial
Passeig de Sant Joan 7
Barcelona, 08010, Spain
Phone: 34-93-303-6820
Fax: 34-93-303-6831
Website: www.norma-ed.es
Email: valiente@normaeditorial.com
Specialty Subjects: Graphic Novels
U.S. Warehouse
Distributors: Public Square Books
Founded 1987 in Spain
Top Authors: Frank Miller, Mike Mignola,
Tadashi Ozawa

Northland Publishing, Inc
2900 N Fort Valley Rd.
Flagstaff, AZ 86001
Phone: 928-774-5251
Fax: 928-774-0592
Website: www.northlandpub.com
Email: info@northlandpub.com
Specialty Subjects: Architecture and Design,
Bilingual Books, Children's Books, Native
American Art, Craft, Culture and History
Imprints: Rising Moon Children's
U.S. Warehouse
Distributors: Baker & Taylor, Brodart, Follett
Library Services, Ingram, Lectorum
U.S. Sales: 99%
Founded 1958 in USA
Top Authors: Bob Wiseman, Linda Kranz,
Susan Lowell

Nuevo Paradigma
San José, Costa Rica
Phone: 506-273-4654
Fax: 506-273-4654
Email: luzvy@racsa.co.cr
Specialty Subjects: Folklore, Self-help,
Textbooks
Founded 2002 in Costa Rica
Top Authors: Carlos Aguilar, Carlos Arauz,
José Angelini

O'Reilly & Associates
1005 Gravenstein Hwy. North
Sebastopol, CA 95472
Phone: 800-998-9938
Fax: 707-829-0104
Website: www.oreilly.com
Email: cindyw@oreilly.com
Specialty Subjects: Computer/Technical
Books
U.S. Warehouse
Founded 1978 in USA

Obelisco Publishing
8871 SW 129 Terrace
Miami, FL 33176
Phone: 866-448-7266
Fax: 305-251-1310
Website: www.edicionesobelisco.com
Email: miami@edicionesurano.com

Specialty Subjects: Alternative Medicine,
Self-help, Spiritual
U.S. Warehouse
Distributors: Advanced Marketing Services,
Anderson Merchandisers, Baker & Taylor,
Bookazine, Brodart, Girón Books, Lectorum,
Libros sin Fronteras, SBD Books, Spanish
Periodicals, The Bilingual Publications Co.
Founded 1981 in Spain
Top Authors: Albert Ellis, Marcia Grad,
Robert Fisher

Ocean Press
PO Box 1186, Old Chelsea Station
New York, NY 10113-1186
Website: www.oceanbooks.com.au
Email: info@oceanbooks.com.au
Specialty Subjects: Biography, History, Latin
America, Politics
U.S. Warehouse
Distributors: Consortium Book Sales &
Distribution
U.S. Sales: 90%
Founded 1989
Top Authors: Che Guevara, Fidel Castro

Pan American Health Organization
525 23rd St. NW
Washington, DC 20037
Phone: 202-974-3049
Fax: 202-338-0869
Website: www.publications.paho.org
Email: pinzonmi@paho.org
Specialty Subjects: Public Health Reference
Books
U.S. Warehouse
Distributors: PMDS
Founded 1902 in USA
Top Authors: Boris Szyfres, Ciro de Quadros,
Pedro N. Acha

Pangaea
226 Wheeler St. South
St. Paul, MN 55105-1927
Phone: 651-690-3320
Fax: 651-690-3320
Website: www.pangaea.org
Email: info@pangaea.org

Specialty Subjects: Bilingual Books on Nature and Indigenous Cultures of the Americas
Imprints: Palm Books
U.S. Warehouse
Distributors: Baker & Taylor, Follett Library Services, IndyBook.com, Ingram, Midwest Library Services, Quality Books, Yankee Book Peddler
U.S. Sales: 75%
Founded 1990 in USA
Top Authors: Alfonso Silva Lee, Carlos Galindo-Leal, Marcelo D. Beccaceci

Parenting Press, Inc.
11065 5th Ave. NE, Suite F
Seattle, WA 98125-6100
Phone: 800-992-6657
Fax: 206-364-0702
Website: www.ParentingPress.com
Email: office@ParentingPress.com
Specialty Subjects: Parenting, Personal Safety for Children
Imprints: Parenting Press
U.S. Warehouse
Distributors: Baker & Taylor, Follett Library Resources, Ingram
U.S. Sales: 95%
Founded 1979 in USA
Top Authors: Diane Davis, Elizabeth Crary, Lory Freeman

Parramón Ediciones, S.A.
Gran Via Corts Catalanes, 322
Barcelona, 08004, Spain
Phone: 34-93-269-2720
Fax: 34-93-426-3730
Website: www.parramon.com
Email: sales@parramon.es

Pathfinder Press
PO Box 162767
Atlanta, GA 162767
Phone: 404-669-0600
Fax: 707-669-1411
Website: www.pathfinderpress.com
Email: orders@pathfinderpress.com
Specialty Subjects: Afro-American Studies, Cuban Revolution, Writing Speeches of Revolutionary Leaders Worldwide, Women's Studies, Working-class Politics and Trade Unions
Imprints: Pathfinder
U.S. Warehouse
Distributors: Self-distributed
Founded 1973 in USA
Top Authors: Friedrich Engels, Karl Marx, Malcolm X

Penguin Young Readers Group
345 Hudson St.
New York, NY 10014
Phone: 212-414-3708
Website: www.penguin.com/youngreaders
Specialty Subjects: Children's and Young Adult Books
Imprints: Dutton Children's Books, GP Putnam's Sons, Viking Children's Books
U.S. Warehouse
Founded 1996 in USA
Top Authors: Eric Carle, Judy Blume, Tomie dePaola

Penton Overseas, Inc.
2470 Impala Dr.
Carlsbad, CA 92008
Phone: 760-431-0060
Fax: 760-431-8110
Website: www.pentonoverseas.com
Email: info@pentonoverseas.com
Specialty Subjects: Children's Educational Material on Audio and DVD, Children's Printed Books, Foreign Language Teaching Materials
Imprints: Smart Kids
U.S. Warehouse
Distributors: Faherty & Associates, McLemore/Hollern & Associates, Melman-Moster Associates, R&R Book Company, The Hopkins Group, Wybel Marketing Group
Founded 1986 in USA

Peterson's–A part of the Thomson Corporation
2000 Lenox Dr.
Lawrenceville, NJ 08648
Phone: 609-896-1800
Fax: 609-896-1811
Website: www.petersons.com

Specialty Subjects: College and Graduate
School Admissions, Distance Learning,
Financial Aid, Test Preparation
U.S. Warehouse
Founded 1966 in USA

Piñata Books
University of Houston, 452 Cullen
Performance Hall
Houston, TX 77204-2004
Phone: 713-743-2999
Fax: 713-743-3080
Website: www.artepublicopress.com
Email: mparle@central.uh.edu
Specialty Subjects: Children and Young
Adult Books
U.S. Warehouse
Distributors: Baker & Taylor, Ingram,
Lectorum
U.S. Sales: 99%
Founded 1994 in USA
Top Authors: Diane Gonzáles, Judith Ortiz
Cofer, Pat Mora

Planeta Publishing Corporation
2057 NW 87th Ave.
Miami, FL 33172
Phone: 800-407-4770
Fax: 305-470-6267
Website: www.planeta.es
Email: infosales@planetapublishing.com
Specialty Subjects: General Trade and
Reference
Imprints: Ariel, Booket, Bronce, CEAC,
Emecé, Joaquín Mortiz, Minotauro, MR,
Plante Junior, Quinteto, Seix Barral, Temas de
Hoy
U.S. Warehouse
Distributors: Baker & Taylor, Bookazine,
Brodart, Follett Library Resources, Lectorum
Founded 1945 in Spain

Playco Editores, C.A.
Calle El Carmen, Centro Dos Caminos
4to. Piso, Oficina 4-B, Los Dos Caminos
Caracas, 1071, Venezuela
Phone: 582-12-235-4736
Fax: 582-12-235-4736
Email: playcoep@cantv.net

Specialty Subjects: Children and Young
Adult Books
U.S. Warehouse
Distributors: Bookspan, Chulainn
Publishing, Distribuidora Cuellar, Donars
Spanish Books, Lectorum, Libros Sin
Fronteras, Mariuccia Iaconi Books Imports,
The Bilingual Publications, VCC Media
U.S. Sales: 15%
Founded 1991 in Venezuela
Top Authors: Aquiles Nazoa, Salvador
Garmendia

Porcia Publishing Corp.
9310 Fontainebleau Blvd., #607
Miami, FL 33172
Phone: 305-364-0035
Fax: 305-551-1658
Email: porciapublishing@bellsouth.net
Specialty Subjects: Metaphysics, New Age,
Spirituality
U.S. Warehouse
Distributors: Downtown Books, Forsa
Editores, Girón, Lectorum, Spanish
Periodicals, World Educational Guild
U.S. Sales: 30%
Founded 1998 in Spain
Top Authors: Annice Booth, Elizabeth Clare
Prophet, Mark L. Prophet

**Promotora de Medios de Comunicación,
S.A.**
Costado Oeste Universidad de Costa Rica
Edificio Electronic Engineering
San José, Costa Rica
Phone: 506-283-3033
Fax: 506-225-1363
Email: edicionespromesa@hotmail.com
Specialty Subjects: Anthropology, Art,
Biography, Education, Family Orientation,
Literature, Poetry, Thoughts, and Creativity
U.S. Sales: 0%
Founded 1982 in Costa Rica
Top Authors: Alfonso López Quintás,
Francisca R. Quiroga, Jutta Burggraf

Publicaciones Alianza
Ciudad de la Paz 2372, 4C
1428CPN Buenos Aires, Argentina
Phone: 54-11-4786-3324

Fax: 54-11-4786-3324
Website: www.publicaciones.net
Email: publicaciones@sion.com
Specialty Subjects: Christian Books
Founded 1991 in Argentina
Top Authors: Betty Constance, Jessica
Ibarbalz, Julio Grasso

Pureplay Press
11353 Missouri Ave.
Los Angeles, CA 90025
Phone: 310-479-8773
Fax: 310-473-9384
Website: www.pureplaypress.com
Email: davidkaori@earthlink.net
Specialty Subjects: Cookbooks, Cuban
Fiction, History, Poetry, Politics, and Culture
U.S. Warehouse
Distributors: Biblio Distribution
U.S. Sales: 100%
Founded 2001 in USA
Top Authors: Enrique Encinosa, Nestor Diaz
de Villegas, Severo Sarduy

Quetzal Publishing Company
521 Admiral's Circle
Pine Beach, NJ 08741
Phone: 732-349-1952
Website: www.jlcarfora.com
Email: inti-ra@litenet.net
Specialty Subjects: Supplemental Grammar
Books
U.S. Warehouse
Founded 1986 in USA

Quill Driver Books
1831 Industrial Way, Suite 101
Sanger, CA 93657
Phone: 559-876-2170
Fax: 559-876-2180
Website: www.QuillDriverBooks.com
Specialty Subjects: Biography, History, How-
to, Parenting, Self-help, Writing, and
Publishing
U.S. Warehouse
Distributors: American West Books, Baker &
Taylor, Ingram, New Leaf, Partners, Quality
Books, Unique Books
Founded 1994 in USA

Quorum Editores
Ancha, 27
Cádiz, Spain
Phone: 34-95-620-5766
Fax: 34-95-626-6533
Website: www.grupoquorum.com
Email: quorumeditores@grupoquorum.com
Specialty Subjects: Gastronomy, Literature,
Medicine, Theater
Founded 1993 in Spain
Top Authors: Félix Palma, Pedro M. Payan
Sotomayor, Pepe Parra

Ra-Ma
Ctra. de Carrillas, 144
Madrid, 28043, Spain
Phone: 34-91-381-0300
Fax: 34-91-381-0372
Website: www.ra-ma.es
Email: editorial@ra-ma.com

Random House Mondadori
1745 Broadway
New York, NY 10019
Phone: 1-212-782-9000 ext. 29116
Fax: 212-940-7381
Website: www.randomhouse.com
Email: cazula@randomhouse.com
Imprints: Debolsillo, Editorial Sudamericana,
Grijalbo, Plaza & Janés
U.S. Warehouse
Founded in México
Top Authors: Esmeralda Santiago, Gabriel
García Márquez, María Antonieta Collins

Random House, Inc.
1745 Broadway
New York, NY 10019
Phone: 212-782-9000
Website: www.randomhouse.com
Imprints: Random House Español
U.S. Warehouse
Distributors: All Major Distributors
Top Authors: Esmeralda Santiago, Gabriel
García Márquez, María Antonieta Collins

Raven Tree Press, LLC
200 South Washington, Suite 306
Green Bay, WI 54301
Phone: 877-256-0579

Fax: 920-438-1607
Website: www.raventreepress.com
Email: dawn@raventreepress.com
Specialty Subjects: Children's Bilingual
Picture Books
Distributors: Baker & Taylor, Ingram
Founded 2000 in USA
Top Authors: Amy Crane Johnson, Lee Bock

RD Editores
San Juan de la Palma, 11
Sevilla, Spain
Phone: 34-95-422-2268
Fax: 34-95-422-1687
Website: www.rdeditores.com
Email: reogeliodelgado@rdeditores.com
Specialty Subjects: General Interest,
Literature
U.S. Warehouse
Distributors: BookSurge
Founded 2000 in Spain
Top Authors: Andrés Sorel, Francisco Robles,
Manuel Mantero

RIL Editores
El Vergel 2882, Oficina 11, Providencia
Santiago, Chile
Phone: 562-223-8100
Fax: 562-225-4269
Website: www.rileditores.com
Email: ril@rileditores.com
Specialty Subjects: Education, Literature,
Social Sciences, Sociology
U.S. Sales: 5%
Founded 1991 in Chile
Top Authors: Alfonso Calderón, Jorge Díaz,
Sergio Villalobos

Riverside Book Company, Inc.
PO Box 237043
New York, NY 10023
Phone: 212-595-0700
Fax: 212-595-0780
Website: www.riversidebook.com
Email: info@riversidebook.com
Specialty Subjects: Illustrated Books on the
Fine Arts, Painters and Sculptors of the
Italian Renaissance
Imprints: Scala/Riverside

U.S. Warehouse
U.S. Sales: 80%
Founded 1987 in USA

**Saber Mountain Publishing Group
International, Inc.**
283 Parr Blvd.
Reno, NV 89512
Phone: 208-365-2218
Website: www.sabermountain.com
Email: donalan@sabermountain.com
Specialty Subjects: Self-help
Imprints: SABER Mountain
U.S. Warehouse
U.S. Sales: 30%
Founded 2002 in USA
Top Authors: Don-Alan Rekow

Santillana USA Publishing Co.
2105 NW 86th Ave.
Miami, FL 33122
Phone: 305-591-9522
Fax: 305-591-7473
Website: www.santillanausa.com
Specialty Subjects: Fiction, Nonfiction.
Imprints: Aguilar, Alamah, Alfaguara, Altea,
Punto de Lectura, Richmond, Taurus
U.S. Warehouse
Distributors: All Major Distributors
Founded 1960 in Spain
Top Authors: Carlos Fuentes, José Saramago,
Mario Vargas Llosa

Sara Jordan Publishing
PO Box 490
Niagara Falls, NY 14302-0490
Phone: 800-567-7733
Fax: 905-938-9970
Website: www.sara-jordan.com
Email: sjordan@s-jordan.com
Specialty Subjects: Curriculum Based/
Linguistics Audio Programs for Children
Imprints: Baker & Taylor, Faithworks,
Ingram
U.S. Warehouse
U.S. Sales: 65%
Founded 1991 in USA
Top Authors: Agustina Tocalli-Beller, Diego
Marulanda, Sara Jordan

Scholastic, Inc.
577 Broadway
New York, NY 10012
Phone: 212-343-6100
Fax: 212-343-6930
Website: www.scholastic.com
Specialty Subjects: Children's Trade,
Nonfiction, Reference Publishing.
Imprints: Arthur A. Levine Books,
Cartwheel Books®, Chicken House™,
Orchard Books®, Scholastic en español,
Scholastic Paperbacks, Scholastic Press,
Scholastic Reference™, The Blue Sky Press®
U.S. Warehouse Distributors: all distributors
Founded 1920 in USA
Top Authors: Dav Pilkey, David Shannon,
Pam Muñoz Ryan

Selector, S.A. de C.V.
Dr. Erazo, 120, Col. Doctores
México City, 06720, México
Phone: 52-55-588-7272
Fax: 52-55-5761-5716
Website: www.selector.com.mx
Email: info@selector.com.mx
Specialty Subjects: Business, Children and
Young Adult Literature, Crafts, Family and
Culture, Health and Beauty, Humor, Science
for Children, Self-help, Self-improvement
Distributors: Girón Books, Lectorum,
Spanish Language Book Services, The
Bilingual Publications Co.
U.S. Sales: 3%
Founded 1949 in México
Top Authors: Abel Cruz, Andrew Mathews,
Mónica Stevens

Self-Realization Fellowship Publishers
3208 Humboldt St.
Los Angeles, CA 90031-1835
Phone: 323-276-6002
Fax: 323-276-6003
Website: www.srfpublishers.org
Email: sales@srfpublishers.org
Specialty Subjects: Inspiration, Religion,
Self-help, Spirituality
U.S. Warehouse
Distributors: Baker & Taylor, Book People,
DeVorss, Ingram, LD Books, New Leaf
U.S. Sales: 10%

Founded 1920 in USA
Top Authors: Paramahansa Yogananda, Sri
Daya Mata

Seven Stories Press/Siete Cuentos Editorial
140 Watts St.
New York, NY 10013
Phone: 212-226-8760
Fax: 212-226-1411
Website: www.sevenstories.com
Email: sara@sevenstories.com
Specialty Subjects: Fiction, Political
Nonfiction
Imprints: Siete Cuentos Editorial
U.S. Warehouse
Distributors: Consortium
U.S. Sales: 75%
Founded 1996 in USA
Top Authors: Ariel Dorfman, Howard Zinn,
Noam Chomsky

Siglo del Hombre Editores, S.A.
Cra. 32 # 25–46
Bogotá, Colombia
Phone: 571-337-7700
Fax: 571-337-7665
Website: www.siglodelhombre.com
Email: gerencia@siglodelhombre.com
Specialty Subjects: Law, Philosophy, Social
Sciences
Founded 1992 in Colombia
Top Authors: Boaventura de Sousa Santos,
Jesús Martín Barbero, Oscar Mejía Quintana

Siglo XXI Editores, S.A. de C.V.
Avda. Cerro del Agua, 248,
Col. Romero de Terreros, Del. Coyoacán
México City, México
Phone: 52-55-565-87-999
Fax: 52-55-565-87-599
Website: www.sigloxxieditores.com.mx
Email: difusion@sigloxxieditores.com.mx
Specialty Subjects: Politics, Sociology.
Distributors: Adalids Foreign Books, Ideal
Foreign Books
Founded 1966 in México
Top Authors: Eduardo Galeano, Michael
Foucault, Roland Barthes

Simon & Schuster
Chidren's Publishing Division
1230 Ave. of the Americas
New York, NY 10020
Phone: 800-223-2336
Fax: 800-943-9831
Website: www.SimonSaysKids.com
Imprints: Libros para Niños
U.S. Warehouse
Founded 1924 in USA

Stampley Enterprises
PO Box 33172
Charlotte, NC 28233
Phone: 704-333-6631
Fax: 704-336-6932
Website: www.stampley.com
Email: info@stampley.com
Specialty Subjects: Children's and Young
Adult Reference, Religion
Imprints: Stampley Enterprises
U.S. Warehouse
Distributors: Girón, Ingram, Lectorum,
Libros Sin Fronteras, Spring Arbor
U.S. Sales: 50%
Founded 1940 in USA

Stockcero, Inc.
2307 Douglas Rd., Suite 400
Miami, FL 33145
Phone: 305-447-8801
Fax: 305-447-8770
Website: www.stockcero.com
Email: info@stockcero.com
Specialty Subjects: Economics, History and
Politics, Literature
Imprints: Stockcero Academic Services
Distributors: Ingram
U.S. Sales: 100%
Founded 2000 in USA
Top Authors: Armando P. Ribas, Cecilia
Absatz, Domingo F. Sarmiento

Swan Isle Press
PO Box 408790
Chicago, IL 60640-8790
Phone: 773-728-3780
Website: www.swanislepress.com
Email: info@swanislepress.com

Specialty Subjects: Fiction, Nonfiction,
Poetry
Imprints: El Cisne Negro Ediciones, La Isla
del Cisne Ediciones
U.S. Warehouse
Distributors: Baker & Taylor, Ingram, The
University of Chicago Press Distribution
Founded 1999 in USA

Taller del Exito, Inc.
1700 NW 65th Ave.
Plantation, FL 33322
Phone: 954-321-5560
Fax: 954-321-5422
Website: www.tallerdelexito.com
Email: ida@elexito.com
Specialty Subjects: Business Excellence,
Leadership, Personal Development
Imprints: Taller del Exito
U.S. Warehouse
Distributors: Agencia de Publicaciones PR,
Bilingual Publications, Books on Wings/
Brodart Español, Cameramundi PR,
Crimson, Follett Multimedia, Girón Books,
Spanish Periodicals
U.S. Sales: 60%
Founded 1994 in USA
Top Authors: Brian Tracy, Dr. Camilo Cruz,
Rafael Ayala

Terranova Editores
PO Box 79509
Carolina, PR 00984-9509
Phone: 787-791-4794
Fax: 787-791-4794
Website: terranovaeditores.tripod.com
Email: eterranova@prtc.net
Specialty Subjects: Narrative, Poetry
U.S. Warehouse
Distributors: Ideal Foreign Books
Founded 2003 in Puerto Rico
Top Authors: Clara Lair, Javier Ávila,
Mercedes López-Baralt

The Learning Light Co.
333 Lewis Ave.
Billings, MA 59101
Phone: 866-391-8901
Website: www.thelearninglight.com
Email: info@thelearninglight.com

Specialty Subjects: Spanish Conversation
U.S. Warehouse
Founded 2000 in USA

Thomson Gale
27500 Drake Rd.
Farmington Hills, MI 48331-3535
Phone: 800-877-4253
Fax: 248-699-8064
Website: www.gale.com
Email: lauri.taylor@thomson.com
Specialty Subjects: Biography, History, Large
Print Fiction, Literature, Medicine,
Nonfiction, Reference, Science, Social Science
Imprints: Blackbirch Press, Thorndike Press
U.S. Warehouse
Distributors: Baker & Taylor, Blackwell,
Brodart, Gale, Ingram
Founded 1954 in USA
Top Authors: Jorge Ramos, Sandra Cisneros,
Tim LaHaye

Time Warner Book Group
1271 Ave. of the Americas
New York, NY 10020
Phone: 212-522-8059
Fax: 212-522-1048
Website: www.twbookmark.com
Email: Melanie.gee@twbg.com
Specialty Subjects: Audiobooks, Business and
Money, Children's Books, Christian, eBooks,
Fantasy, Fiction, Mystery, Nonfiction,
Romance, Science Fiction, Self-help, Teen
Reads, Arts
Imprints: Aspect, Back Bay, Brown &
Company, Bulfinch, Children's Books, Little,
Mysterious Press, Time Warner Audiobooks,
Warner Books, Warner Business Books,
Warner Forever
U.S. Warehouse
Founded 1970 in USA
Top Authors: Joyce Meyer, Robert Kiyosaki,
Rudolfo Anaya

Trident Press International
801 12th Ave. South, Suite 400
Naples, FL 34102
Phone: 239-649-7077
Fax: 239-649-5832
Website: www.trident-international.com

Email: sales@trident-international.com
Specialty Subjects: Cookbooks, Dictionaries,
Encyclopedias, Military
U.S. Warehouse
U.S. Sales: 60%
Founded 1992 in USA

Turner Publicaciones, S.L.
c/Rafael Calvo, 42
Escalera Izquierda, 2™ Planta
Madrid, Spain
Phone: 34-91-308-33-36
Fax: 34-91-319-39-30
Website: www.turnerlibros.com
Email: turner@turnerlibros.com
Specialty Subjects: Art Philosophy,
Bullfighting, Illustrated Art and Photography
Books, Literary Reviews, Music, Nonfiction
Imprints: Turner
Distributors: DAP
Founded 1973 in Spain

Turtle Books
866 United Nations Plaza, #525
New York, NY 10017
Phone: 212 644 2020
Fax: 212-223-4387
Website: www.turtlebooks.com
Email: turtlebook@aol.com
Specialty Subjects: Children's Picture Books
Imprints: Turtle Books, Turtle Media
U.S. Warehouse
Distributors: Publishers Group West
U.S. Sales: 90%
Founded 1996 in USA
Top Authors: Daniel Moreton, Jo Harper,
Robert Casilla

Tusquets/Urano Publishing
8871 SW 129 Terrace
Miami, FL 33176
Phone: 305-233-3365
Fax: 305-251-1310
Website: www.edicionesurano.com
Email: lucia@edicionesurano.com
Specialty Subjects: Authentic Spanish
literature including Memoir, Biography,
Fiction, History, Poetry, and Children's
Literature
U.S. Warehouse

Distributors: Baker & Taylor, The Bilingual Publications Co., Bookazine, Brodart, Girón Spanish Books, Lectorum, Libros Sin Fronteras, SBD Books, Spanish Periodicals, Anderson Merchandisers
Founded 1964 in Spain

Universidad del País Vasco
Apartado. 1397
Bilbao, 48980, Spain
Phone: 34-94-601-5126
Fax: 34-94-480-1314
Website: www.ehu.es/servicios/se_az
Email: luxedito@lg.ehu.es
Specialty Subjects: University Books
Distributors: Celesa
U.S. Sales: 3%
Founded 1982 in Spain

Urano Publishing, Inc.
8871 SW 129 Terrace
Miami, FL 33176
Phone: 305-233-3365
Fax: 305-251-1310
Website: www.edicionesurano.com
Email: lucia@edicionesurano.com
Specialty Subjects: Alternative Medicine, Applied Psychology, Astrology, Biographies, Business, Fiction, Children's and Young Adult Literature, Current Events, Fiction, History, Memoirs, Personal Growth, Poetry, Romance Novels, Spiritual and New Age.
Imprints: Empresa Activa, Titania, Umbriel, Urano
U.S. Warehouse
Distributors: Anderson, Baker & Taylor, Bookazine, Brodart, Girón, Lectorum, Libros Sin Fronteras, SBD Books, Spanish Periodical, The Bilingual Publications Co.
U.S. Sales: 10%
Founded 1969 in Spain
Top Authors: Dan Brown, Linda Howard, Spencer Johnson

Velazquez Press
9682 Telstar Ave., Suite 110
El Monte, CA 91731
Phone: 626-448-3448
Fax: 626-602-3817
Website: www.VelazquezPress.com

Email: info@AcademicLearningCompany.com
Specialty Subjects: Reference
Imprints: Velazquez Press
U.S. Warehouse
Distributors: Baker & Taylor, Follet, Ingram
U.S. Sales: 90%
Founded in USA

Vergara y Riba Editoras, S.A.
Ayacucho 1920
Buenos Aires, 1112, Argentina
Phone: 54-11-4807-4664
Fax: 54-11-4807-4664
Website: www.vergarariba.com.ar
Email: editoras@vergarariba.com.ar
Specialty Subjects: Gift Books
Distributors: Perrone Importers
U.S. Sales: 5%
Founded 1996 in Argentina
Top Authors: Mario Benedetti, Pablo Neruda, Paulo Coelho

Versal Editorial Group, Inc.
10 High St.
Andover, MA 01810
Phone: 978-470-1972
Fax: 978-470-3812
Website: www.versalgroup.com
Email: RigoAguirre@versalgroup.com
Specialty Subjects: All Genres, Fiction and Nonfiction
Imprints: Abalorios Collection, Aleteos Collection, Colorin Colorado Collection, En Letra Mayscula Collection, Esencias Collection, Himalaya Collection, Palco Reservado Collection
U.S. Warehouse
U.S. Sales: 100%
Founded 1994 in USA
Top Authors: Emilio Bejel, Gastón Alvaro Santana, Yanitzia Canetti

Villegas Editores, S.A.
Av 82 11–50, Interior 3
Bogotá, Colombia
Phone: 571-616-1788
Fax: 571-616-0020
Website: www.villegaseditores.com
Email: informacion@villegaseditores.com

Specialty Subjects: High-end Illustrated
Books
Distributors: Rizzoli International
U.S. Sales: 7%
Founded 1985 in Colombia
Top Authors: Carlos Fuentes, Gerardo
Reichel Dolmatoff, Richard Evans Schultes

Vincero Enterprises
490 Marin Oaks Dr.
Novato, CA 94949-5467
Phone: 800-715-1492
Fax: 415-883-4115
Website: www.hispaniclatino.net
Email: heritage1492@earthlink.net
Specialty Subjects: Bilingual Cultural
Compendiums
Imprints: Patrimonio Hispanoamericano,
Patrimonio Italo Americano
U.S. Warehouse
Distributors: Applause Learning Resources,
Baker & Taylor, Ingram, Libros Sin Fronteras,
Quality Books, SBD Spanish Book
Distributors, TyERA Co.
Founded 1999 in USA
Top Authors: Leon J. Radomile

Vintage Books & Anchor Books /
Vintage Español
1745 Broadway
New York, NY 10019
Phone: 212-782-9000
Fax: 212-572-6043
Website: www.randomhouse.com/vintage/
Email:
vintageanchorpublicity@randomhouse.com
Specialty Subjects: General Nonfiction,
Literary Fiction, Memoir
Imprints: Vintage Español
U.S. Warehouse
Founded in USA
Top Authors: Gabriel García Márquez, Laura
Esquivel, Sandra Cisneros

Wellesworth Publishing
PO Box 372444
Satellite Beach, FL 32937
Phone: 321-779-9999
Fax: 321-779-3333

Website: www.wellesworth.com
Email: marymc@cfl.r.com
Specialty Subjects: Reference
U.S. Warehouse
Distributors: Baker & Taylor, Brodart,
Quality Books
U.S. Sales: 90%
Founded 1997 in USA

WPR Publishing
2107 Carlsbad Village Dr., Suite D
Carlsbad, CA 92008
Phone: 760-434-7474
Fax: 760-434-7476
Website: www.latinoprintnetwork.com
Email: laura@latinoprintnetwork.com
Specialty Subjects: Hispanic Research and
Directories
U.S. Warehouse
U.S. Sales: 98%
Founded 1996 in USA

Your Business
21820 Marylee St., Suite 226
Woodland Hills, CA 91367
Phone: 818-999-4000
Fax: 818-999-4000
Website: businessbyyou.com
Email: mirta@businessbyyou.com
Specialty Subjects: Self-help, Spiritual
Distributors: Baker & Taylor, Book Clearing
House
U.S. Sales: 90%
Founded 2003 in USA
Top Authors: Mabel Katz

Yoyo USA, Inc.
20326 NE 16th Place
North Miami Beach, FL 33179
Phone: 305-652-1444
Fax: 305-652-1334
Website: www.yoyousa.com
Email: info@yoyousa.com
Specialty Subjects: Adventure, Children's and
Young Adult, Classics, Fantasy, Historical
Fiction, Horror, Humor, Romance, Science
Fiction, Self-help
U.S. Warehouse
Founded 1997

Audio Publishers

Barefoot Books
2067 Massachusetts Ave.
Cambridge, MA 02140
Phone: 617-576-0660
Fax: 617-576-0049
Website: www.barefootbooks.com
Email: ussales@barefootbooks.com
Specialty Subjects: Multiculturalism
U.S. Warehouse
Distributors: Baker & Taylor, Book
Wholesalers Inc., Follett, Ingram
U.S. Sales: 70%
Founded 1993 in United Kingdom
Top Authors: Mary Finch, Mary-Joan
Gerson, Stella Blackstone.

Bilingual Books, Inc.
1719 W Nickerson St.
Seattle, WA 98119
Phone: 800-488-5068
Fax: 206-284-3660
Website: www.bbks.com
Email: info@bbks.com
Specialty Subjects: Audio CD Titles, ESL
Instruction Books, Phrase Guides, Spanish
Instruction Books.
U.S. Warehouse
Distributors: Baker & Taylor, Ingram, West
Book Distributing, Inc.
Founded 1981 in USA

Bridge Publications
4751 Fountain Ave.
Los Angeles, CA 90029
Phone: 323-953-3320
Fax: 323-953-3328
Website: www.bridgepub.com
Email: info@bridgepub.com
Specialty Subjects: Health and Fitness,
Religious, Self-help, Spirituality
U.S. Warehouse
Distributors: Baker & Taylor, Ingram
U.S. Sales: 95%
Founded 1981 in USA
Top Authors: L. Ron Hubbard

Broadman & Holman Publishers
127 9th Ave. North
Nashville, TN 37234
Phone: 800-251-3225
Fax: 615-251-2469
Website: www.broadmanholman.com
Specialty Subjects: Bibles, Biblical
References, Inspirational, Religious
Imprints: B & H Español
U.S. Warehouse
Distributors: Baker & Taylor, Ingram
Founded 1801 in USA
Top Authors: Beth Moore, Jerry Jenkins, Tim
LaHayes

Bull Publishing
PO Box 1377
Boulder, CO 80306
Phone: 800-676-2855
Specialty Subjects: Medical, Nutrition, Self-
help, Sports Medicine
Distributors: Publishers Group West
U.S. Sales: 90%
Founded 1973 in USA
Top Authors: Deborah Stewart, Kate Lorig

Cantemos
15696 Altamira Dr.
Chino Hills, CA 91709
Phone: 800-393-1336
Fax: 909-393-1362
Websites: www.cantemosco.com and
www.simplespanishsongs.com
Email: jarjetb@aol.com
Specialty Subjects: Songs in Spanish from
Latin America.
U.S. Warehouse
Distributors: Baker & Taylor, Follet Library
Resources
U.S. Sales: 100%
Founded 1991 in USA
Top Authors: Michael Mastorakis

Coral Communications Group, LLC
880 Fifth Ave., Suite 8F
New York, NY 10021
Phone: 212-249-8733
Fax: 212-744-7090
Website: www.coralcomm.com
Email: coralcom@worldnet.att.net
Specialty Subjects: Audiobooks in Spanish, Latin American Fiction, Self-help
Imprints: Audiolibros Nueva Onda
U.S. Warehouse
Distributors: AudioForum, Libros Sin Fronteras, The Bilingual Publications Co.
U.S. Sales: 95%
Founded 1989 in USA
Top Authors: Frank Rivera, Jorge Covarrubias, Mariano Azuela

Early Advantage
79 Sanford St.
Fairfield, CT 06824
Phone: 888-327-5923
Fax: 800-409-9928
Website: www.early-advantage.com
Email: lynnj@early-advantage.com
Specialty Subjects: ESL, Foreign Language, History, Language Arts, Music
U.S. Warehouse
Founded in USA

Edibesa
Calle Madre de Dios, 35
Madrid, 28016, Spain
Phone: 34-91-345-1992
Fax: 34-91-350-5099
Website: www.edibesa.com
Email: edibesa@planalfa.es
Specialty Subjects: Religion
U.S. Sales: 5%
Founded 1984 in Spain
Top Authors: François Mauriac, José María Pemán, Juan Pablo II

Editorial Océano de México, S.A. de C.V.
Eugenio Sue # 59
Col. Chapultepec Polanco
Deleg. Miguel Hidalgo
México City, México
Phone: 52-55-5279-9000

Fax: 52-55-5279-9006
Website: www.oceano.com.mx
Email: export@oceano.com.mx
Specialty Subjects: Biography, Children's and Young Adult, Dictionaries, Novels, Photography/Art, Politics, Self-help, Classics
Imprints: Abraxas, Americo Arte, Circe, Lengua de Trapo, Losada, Océano, Océano Ambar, Océano CONACULTA, Océano Turner, Salamandra, Turner.
U.S. Warehouse
Distributors: All Major U.S. Distributors
U.S. Sales: 15%
Founded 1988 in México
Top Authors: Guadalupe Loaeza, Luis Spota, Sara Sefchovich

Educational Services Corporation
PO Box 797
Rockville, MD 20848-0797
Phone: 301-374-9008
Fax: 301-374-2216
U.S. Warehouse
Distributors: Ingram
U.S. Sales: 90%
Founded 1948 in USA

Edufam Ediciones S.A. de C.V.
Maximino A. Camacho 63-1
Col. Nápoles, Deleg. Benito Juárez, C.P.
México City, 03810, México
Phone: 5563-1558
Fax: 5611-8978
Email: edufammx@yahoo.com
Specialty Subjects: Religion, Self-improvement, Technology
Founded 2001 in México
Top Authors: Carlos Alvear García García, María Icaza, Manuel Jiménez

Fondo de Cultura Económica USA, Inc.
2293 Vreus St.
San Diego, CA 92154
Phone: 619-429-0455
Fax: 619-429-0827
Website: www.fceusa.com
Email: sales@fceusa.com
Specialty Subjects: Anthropology, Art, Children's Literature, History, Literary

Reviews, Mexican and Latin American Literature, Politics and Economics, Science
U.S. Warehouse
Distributors: Adler's Foreign Books, Atanasio & Associates, Baker & Taylor, Brodart, Mariuccia Iaconi Book Imports, Ideal Foreign Books, Ingram, Lectorum, Libros Sin Fronteras
U.S. Sales: 5%
Founded 1934 in México
Top Authors: Juan Rulfo, Octavio Paz, Rosario Castellanos

FonoLibro, Inc.
PO Box 226977
Miami, FL 33172
Phone: 305-718-8108
Fax: 305-718-4280
Website: www.fonolibro.com
Email: info@fonolibro.com
Specialty Subjects: Fiction Audiobooks
Imprints: FonoLibro
U.S. Warehouse
Distributors: Baker & Taylor, Downtown Book Center
U.S. Sales: 95%
Founded 2003 in USA
Top Authors: Bernardo Guimaraes, J.J. Benítez, Rómulo Gallegos

Guilford Publications
72 Spring St.
New York, NY 10012
Phone: 212-431-9800
Fax: 212-966-6708
Website: www.guilford.com
Email: info@guilford.com
Specialty Subjects: Trade and Professional Books in Psychology, Psychiatry, Behavioral Sciences, Education, Geography and Communications
Imprints: Guilford Press
U.S. Warehouse
Distributors: Academic Book Center, Baker & Taylor, Blackwell's Book Services, Book House, Brodart, Coutts Library Services, Eastern Book Co., Ingram Book Co., JA Majors, Matthews Book Co., MBS Book Exchange, Mid-West Library Service,

NACSCORP, Rittenhouse, Yankee Book Peddler
Founded 1973 in USA
Top Authors: Christine Padesky, Jose Bauermeister, Russell Barkley

HarperCollins Publishers-Rayo
10 E 53rd St.
New York, NY 10022
Phone: 212-207-7787
Fax: 212-207-6978
Website: www.HarperCollins.com
Email: JeanMarie.Kelly@HarperCollins.com
Specialty Subjects: Children's Nonfiction, Children's fiction, General Fiction, Nonfiction
Imprints: Rayo
U.S. Warehouse
Founded 1997 in USA
Top Authors: Isabel Allende, Jorge Ramos, Paulo Coelho

Liturgical Press
St John's Abbey
Collegeville, MN 656321
Phone: 800-858-5450
Fax: 800-445-5899
Website: www.litpress.org
Email: sales@litpress.org
Specialty Subjects: Liturgy, Monasticism, Spirituality, Theology
Imprints: Michael Glazier, Pueblo Books
U.S. Warehouse
Distributors: Baker & Taylor, Ingram
U.S. Sales: 85%
Founded 1926 in USA

Penton Overseas, Inc.
2470 Impala Dr.
Carlsbad, CA 92008
Phone: 760-431-0060
Fax: 760-431-8110
Website: www.pentonoverseas.com
Email: info@pentonoverseas.com
Specialty Subjects: Children's Educational Material on Audio and DVD, Children's Books, Foreign Language Teaching Materials
Imprints: Smart Kids
U.S. Warehouse

Distributors: Faherty & Associates, McLemore/Hollern & Associates, Melman-Moster Associates, R&R Book Company, The Hopkins Group, Wybel Marketing Group
Founded 1986 in USA

Recorded Books
270 Skipjack Rd.
Prince Frederick, MD
Phone: 800-638-1304
Fax: 410-535-5499
Website: www.recordedbooks.com
Email: libraries@recordedbooks.com
Specialty Subjects: British, Children/Young Adult, Contemporary African American Fiction, Inspirational, Romance, Self-help
U.S. Warehouse
U.S. Sales: 100%
Founded 1979 in USA
Top Authors: Alexander McCall Smith, Mark Haddon, Shirley Hazzard

Sara Jordan Publishing
PO Box 490
Niagara Falls, NY 14302-0490
Phone: 800-567-7733
Fax: 905-938-9970
Website: www.sara-jordan.com
Email: sjordan@s-jordan.com
Specialty Subjects: Curriculum Based/Linguistics Audio Programs for Children
Imprints: Baker & Taylor, Faithworks, Ingram
U.S. Warehouse
U.S. Sales: 65%
Founded 1991 in USA
Top Authors: Agustina Tocalli-Beller, Diego Marulanda, Sara Jordan.

Taller del Exito, Inc.
1700 NW 65th Ave
Plantation, FL 33322
Phone: 954-321-5560
Fax: 954-321-5422
Website: www.tallerdelexito.com
Email: ida@elexito.com
Specialty Subjects: Business Excellence, Leadership, Personal Development
Imprints: Taller del Exito
U.S. Warehouse

Distributors: Agencia de Publicaciones PR, Bilingual Publications, Brodart Español, Cameramundi PR, Crimson, Follett Multimedia, Girón Books, Spanish Periodicals
U.S. Sales: 60%
Founded 1994 in USA
Top Authors: Brian Tracy, Dr. Camilo Cruz, Rafael Ayala

The Learning Light Co.
333 Lewis Ave.
Billings, MA 59101
Phone: 866-391-8901
Website: www.thelearninglight.com
Email: info@thelearninglight.com
Specialty Subjects: Spanish Conversation
U.S. Warehouse
Founded 2000 in USA

Weston Woods Studios
143 Main St.
Norwalk, CT 06851
Phone: 800-243-5020
Fax: 203-845-0498
Website: www.scholastic.com/westonwoods
Email: lcorra@scholastic.com
Specialty Subjects: Children's Books
Imprints: Weston Woods Studios
U.S. Warehouse
Distributors: Baker & Taylor, Follett, Library Video, Midwest Tape
U.S. Sales: 90%
Founded 1953 in USA
Top Authors: Maurice Sendak, Robert McCloskey, William Steig

Yoyo USA, Inc.
20326 NE 16th Place
North Miami Beach, FL 33179
Phone: 305-652-1444
Fax: 305-652-1334
Website: www.yoyousa.com
Email: info@yoyousa.com
Specialty Subjects: Adventure, Children's and Young Adult, Classics, Fantasy, Historical Fiction, Horror, Humor, Romance, Science Fiction, Self-help
U.S. Warehouse
Founded 1997

Video Publishers

Active Parenting Publishers
1955 Vaughn Rd. NW, Suite 108
Kennesaw, GA 30144-7808
Phone: 800-825-0060
Fax: 770-429-0334
Website: www.activeparenting.com
Email: cservice@activeparenting.com
Specialty Subjects: Parenting
U.S. Warehouse
U.S. Sales: 98%
Founded 1983 in USA
Top Authors: Betsy Gard, Ph.D., Marilyn
Montgomery, Ph.D., Michael H. Popkins,
Ph.D.

Bridge Publications
4751 Fountain Ave.
Los Angeles, CA 90029
Phone: 323-953-3320
Fax: 323-953-3328
Website: www.bridgepub.com
Email: info@bridgepub.com
Specialty Subjects: Health and Fitness,
Religious, Self-help, Spirituality
U.S. Warehouse
Distributors: Baker & Taylor, Ingram
U.S. Sales: 95%
Founded 1981 in USA
Top Authors: L. Ron Hubbard

Discovery Channel School
One Discovery Place
Silver Spring, MD 20910
Phone: 240-662-2000
Fax: 240-662-1979
Website: www.discoveryschool.com
Email: Trisha_Roberts@discovery.com
Specialty Subjects: Geography, History,
Science
U.S. Warehouse
U.S. Sales: 100%
Founded 1989 in USA

Early Advantage
79 Sanford St.
Fairfield, CT 06824
Phone: 888-327-5923
Fax: 800-409-9928
Website: www.early-advantage.com
Email: lynnj@early-advantage.com
Specialty Subjects: ESL, Foreign Language,
History, Language Arts, Music
U.S. Warehouse
Founded in USA

**Editorial INBio (Editorial del Instituto
Nacional de Biodiversidad)**
Del Cementerio de Santo Domingo
1 Bloque al Norte y Dos al Oeste
Heredia, Costa Rica
Phone: 506-507-8184
Fax: 506-507-8274
Website: www.inbio.ac.cr/editorial
Email: editorial@inbio.ac.cr
Specialty Subjects: Nature
U.S. Sales: 50%
Founded 2001 in Costa Rica
Top Authors: Dr. Barry Hammel, Dr. Garret
Crow, Dr. Ginber Garrison

Edufam Ediciones S.A. de C.V.
Maximino A. Camacho 63-1
Col. Nápoles, Deleg., Benito Juárez, C.P.
México City, 03810, México
Phone: 52-55-563-1558
Fax: 52-55-561-8978
Email: edufammx@yahoo.com
Specialty Subjects: Religion, Self-
improvement, Technology
Founded 2001 in México
Top Authors: Carlos Alvear García, María
Icaza, Manuel Jiménez

Films for the Humanities & Sciences
PO Box 2053
Princeton, NJ 08534-2053
Phone: 800-257-5126
Fax: 609-671-5777

Website: www.films.com
Email: custserv@films.com
Specialty Subjects: Culture, Literature, Spanish and Latin American Videos
U.S. Warehouse
U.S. Sales: 95%
Founded 1959 in USA
Top Authors: Diego Velázquez, Frida Kahlo, NAFTA and the New Economic Frontier

Fondo de Cultura Económica USA, Inc.
2293 Vreus St.
San Diego, CA 92154
Phone: 619-429-0455
Fax: 619-429-0827
Website: www.fceusa.com
Email: sales@fceusa.com
Specialty Subjects: Anthropology, Art, Children's Literature, History, Literary Reviews, Mexican and Latin American Literature, Politics and Economics, Science
U.S. Warehouse
Distributors: Adler's Foreign Books, Atanasio & Associates, Baker & Taylor, Brodart, Mariuccia Iaconi Book Imports, Ideal Foreign Books, Ingram, Lectorum, Libros Sin Fronteras
U.S. Sales: 5%
Founded 1934 in México
Top Authors: Juan Rulfo, Octavio Paz, Rosario Castellanos

Guilford Publications
72 Spring St.
New York, NY 10012
Phone: 212-431-9800
Fax: 212-966-6708
Website: www.guilford.com
Email: info@guilford.com
Specialty Subjects: Trade and Professional Books in Psychology, Psychiatry, Behavioral Sciences, Education, Geography and Communications
Imprints: Guilford Press
U.S. Warehouse
Distributors: Academic Book Center, Baker & Taylor, Blackwell's Book Services, Book House, Brodart, Coutts Library Services, Eastern Book Co., Ingram Book Co., JA Majors, Matthews Book Co., MBS Book Exchange, Mid-West Library Service,

NACSCORP, Rittenhouse, Yankee Book Peddler
Founded 1973 in USA
Top Authors: Christine Padesky, Jose Bauermeister, Russell Barkley

Liturgical Press
St John's Abbey
Collegeville, MN 65321
Phone: 800-858-5450
Fax: 800-445-5899
Website: www.litpress.org
Email: sales@litpress.org
Specialty Subjects: Liturgy, Monasticism, Spirituality, Theology
Imprints: Michael Glazier, Pueblo Books
U.S. Warehouse
Distributors: Baker & Taylor, Ingram
U.S. Sales: 85%
Founded 1926 in USA

Nest Family
PO Box 322
Grafton, MA 01519
Phone: 800-988-6378
Fax: 508-887-9755
Website: www.charactered.com
Email: fammedia@aol.com
Specialty Subjects: Animated Historical Heroes, Bible Collection
U.S. Warehouse
Founded in USA

Weston Woods Studios
143 Main St.
Norwalk, CT 06851
Phone: 800-243-5020
Fax: 203-845-0498
Website: www.scholastic.com/westonwoods
Email: lcorra@scholastic.com
Specialty Subjects: Children's Books
Imprints: Weston Woods Studios
U.S. Warehouse
Distributors: Baker & Taylor, Follett, Library Video, Midwest Tape
U.S. Sales: 90%
Founded 1953 in USA
Top Authors: Maurice Sendak, Robert McCloskey, William Steig

Notes

FOREWORD

1. Ghada Elturk, "Diversity and Cultural Competency,"*Colorado Libraries* (Winter 2003): 5-7.
2. Isabel Espinal. "Wanted Latino Librarians," *Críticas, An English Speaker's Guide to the Latest Spanish Language Titles*, September/October 2003, Vol. 3, No. 5.

CHAPTER 1

1. Roberto R. Ramirez and G. Patricia de la Cruz, 2002, *The Hispanic Population in the United States: March 2002* (Washington DC: Current Population Reports, P20-545, U.S. Census Bureau, 2002).
   Available at www.census.gov/prod/2003pubs/p20-545.pdf
2. Roberto R. Ramirez and G. Patricia de la Cruz, 2002, *The Hispanic Population in the United States: March 2002* (Washington DC: Current Population Reports, P20-545, U.S. Census Bureau, 2002).
   Available at www.census.gov/prod/2003pubs/p20-545.pdf
3. Roberto Suro and Jeffrey S. Passel, October 2003, *The Rise of the Second Generation: Changing Patterns in Latino Population Growth* (Washington DC: A Pew Hispanic Center Study, A Project of the Pew Charitable Trusts and USC Annenberg School for Communication, 2003).
   Available at www.pewhispanic.org/reports/archive/
4. Mollyann Brodie, Ph.D. et al, *2002 National Survey of Latinos* (Washington DC and Menlo Park, CA: Pew Hispanic Center/Kaiser Family Foundation, 2002).
   Available at www.pewhispanic.org/reports/archive/
5. Marcelo M. Suárez-Orozco, "Everything You Ever Wanted to Know About Assimilation But Were Afraid to Ask," *Daedalus, Journal of the American Academy of Arts and Sciences* (2000, Fall Volume 129, Number 4): 1-30.
6. *Marketing to the U.S. Hispanic Population, Part I: An Overview* (Magnet Communications, 2002).
   Available at www.hispanicprwire.com/images/images_2002/HispanicMarketing.pdf
7. Pat Mora, *The Rainbow Tulip* (New York, NY: Viking Books, 1999).
8. Mollyann Brodie, Ph.D. et al, *2002 National Survey of Latinos* (Washington DC and Menlo Park, CA: Pew Hispanic Center/Kaiser Family Foundation, 2002).
   Available at www.pewhispanic.org/reports/archive/
9. *1997 Economic Census, Minority- and Women-Owned Businesses, United States* (Washington DC: U.S. Census Bureau).
   Available at www.census.gov/epcd/mwb97/us/us.html#PDF
10. *Census 2000* (Washington DC: U.S. Census Bureau). Available at www.census.gov
11. *comScore Media Metrix Hispanic Services* (Restson, Virginia: comScore Networks, 2003).
12. "Surveying the Digital Future," *UCLA Internet Report Report-Year 3* (Los Angeles, California: UCLA Center for Communication Policy, 2003).
13. Ghada Elturk, "Diversity and Cultural Competency,"*Colorado Libraries* (Winter 2003): 5-7.

CHAPTER 2

1. Ghada Kanafani Elturk. "Public Libraries and Improved Service to Diverse Communities," in *Library Services to Latinos: An Anthology*, ed. Salvador Güereña (Jefferson, North Carolina and London: McFarland & Company, Inc., 2000).

CHAPTER 3

1. "Tours of the Library for Spanish Speakers: Why and How?" *Public Libraries Using Spanish*, www.sol-plus.net/plus/outreach/tours.htm.
2. "Tours of the Library for Spanish Speakers: Why and How?" *Public Libraries Using Spanish*, www.sol-plus.net/plus/outreach/tours.htm.
3. Joe Hayes, *Here Comes the Storyteller* (El Paso, Texas: Cinco Puntos Press, 1996).
4. Dick Keis, "Building Community with Books: A Case Study of the Libros y Familias Program," in *Community Partnerships*, ed. Elsa Auerbach (Alexandria, Virginia: Teachers of English to Speakers of Other Languages, Inc., 2002).
5. Bruce Jenson, "ESL classes can magnetize your library for new users," *Public Libraries Using Spanish*, www.sol-plus.net/plus/outreach/tours.htm.
6. Ghada Kanafani Elturk. "Public Libraries and Improved Service to Diverse Communities," in *Library Services to Latinos: An Anthology*, ed. Salvador Güereña (Jefferson, North Carolina and London: McFarland & Company, Inc., 2000).
7. Ghada Kanafani Elturk. "Public Libraries and Improved Service to Diverse Communities," in *Library Services to Latinos: An Anthology*, ed. Salvador Güereña (Jefferson, North Carolina and London: McFarland & Company, Inc., 2000).
8. Ghada Kanafani Elturk. "Public Libraries and Improved Service to Diverse Communities," in *Library Services to Latinos: An Anthology*, ed. Salvador Güereña (Jefferson, North Carolina and London: McFarland & Company, Inc., 2000).

CHAPTER 5

1. Isabel Espinal. "Wanted Latino Librarians," *Críticas, An English Speaker's Guide to the Latest Spanish Language Titles*, September/October 2003, Vol. 3, No. 5.